The economic rise of early America

The discovery of America, and that of a passage to the East Indies by the Cape of Good Hope, are the two greatest and most important events recorded in the history of mankind. Their consequences have already been very great: but in the short period of between two and three centuries which has elapsed since these discoveries were made, it is impossible that the whole extent of their consequences can have been seen. What benefits, or what misfortunes to mankind may hereafter result from those great events, no human wisdom can foresee. By uniting, in some measure, the most distant parts of the world, by enabling them to relieve one another's wants, to increase one another's enjoyments, and to encourage one another's industry, their general tendency would seem to be beneficial.

Adam Smith, *An Inquiry into
the Nature and Causes of the WEALTH OF NATIONS, 1776*
(New York: The Modern Library, 1937), p. 590.

The economic rise of early America

GARY M. WALTON

Washington State University, Pullman, Washington

JAMES F. SHEPHERD

Whitman College, Walla Walla, Washington

CAMBRIDGE UNIVERSITY PRESS

CAMBRIDGE

LONDON   NEW YORK   MELBOURNE

Published by the Syndics of the Cambridge University Press
The Pitt Building, Trumpington Street, Cambridge CB2 1RP
Bentley House, 200 Euston Road, London NW1 2DB
32 East 57th Street, New York, NY 10022, USA
296 Beaconsfield Parade, Middle Park, Melbourne 3206, Australia

First published 1979

Printed in the United States of America
Typeset by Huron Valley Graphics, Ann Arbor, Michigan
Printed and bound by Hamilton Printing Company, Rensselear, New York

Library of Congress Cataloging in Publication Data

Walton, Gary M.
The economic rise of early America.

Bibliography: p.

Includes index.

1. United States –Commerce –History.
2. Great Britain –Colonies –America –Commerce.
I. Shepherd, James F., joint author.   II.   Title.
HF3025.W34   380.1 0 973   78-13438
ISBN 0 521 22282 6 hard cover
ISBN 0 521 29433 9 paperback

FOR OUR SONS, WITH AFFECTION AND PRIDE

Surrey Max Walton
Devon Brock Walton
Rhodes Laramie Walton
Stephen Donald Shepherd
James F. Shepherd, III
John Michael Shepherd
Joseph Daniel Shepherd

CONTENTS

PREFACE

It has now been more than a decade since Douglass North labeled the colonial period "nearly a void as far as any economic analysis is concerned."[1] In the last dozen years much effort has been marshaled to lessen our ignorance of the economic history of the British North American colonies. It is not appropriate at this point to list the many important contributions that have appeared during this interim, but these along with older, established studies are presented below in footnote citations and in selected references at the end of chapters. The important point is that the abundance of recent research on the colonial period has not yet been widely disseminated in the classrooms, through textbooks, other readings, or in lectures.

The Economic Rise of Early America is a step toward communicating the many scholarly findings that have recently vitalized the subject of economic change in early America. Obviously the book does not provide an exhaustive and complete general economic history of the colonies. Our approach has been deliberately selective, and by design the book is intended as a supplement to larger texts on U.S. economic history. In short, it is aimed at extending our understanding of the critical forces of economic change in early America by concentrating on the several key economic issues of that period.

The theoretical framework of the book is straightforward, although it has been maintained in narrative form and with-

[1]Douglass C. North, "The State of Economic History," *American Economic Review*, LV, 2 (May 1965), p. 88.

out use of abstraction. The focus is on the commercial sector and how it provided the initial driving force for economic growth and development in the colonies. Because of their importance, therefore, the variety of external economic relations of the colonies are given primary attention.

Technical terms and economic jargon have been kept to a minimum and where first used they are identified and defined in a glossary of terms at the end of the text. We hope that by doing this, needed clarity is maintained without loss of readability.

We are grateful to many colleagues for their advice and encouragement: Fred Bateman, Stuart Bruchey, Philip Coelho, Stanley L. Engerman, Albert Fishlow, Robert W. Fogel, Alice Hanson Jones, Lawrence A. Harper, Gloria L. Main, Jackson Turner Main, Russell R. Menard, Irene Niu, Douglass C. North, Jack J. Purdum, Roger L. Ransom, Harry Scheiber, R.L. Sexton, Richard Sutch, Mary Yeager, and others. Working as an editorial and production team were Linda Parker and Linda K. Olson, and Marion Impola contributed greatly to the literary quality of the book. We are grateful also to the Guggenheim Foundation for support for Gary M. Walton, and to Whitman College for support for James F. Shepherd, for parts of this study. Lastly, we appreciate the permission of *Explorations in Economic History* and the *Journal of Economic History* to reprint portions of our research that have already appeared in article form.

Gary M. Walton
James F. Shepherd

1

Introduction

Far from American shores, two great nations were standing on the brink of war. The year was 1793, and the onslaught was about to produce surprising results in the economic development of the newborn United States. Once the first shot was fired, Britain and France launched a protracted series of hostilities that was interrupted only one time (1801–3) in the weary twenty-two years before peace was finally reached. During the long struggle, British and French ships that formerly had carried peacetime cargo were drafted into war service, and the belligerents quickly had to relax the trade restrictions that had formerly been protecting their merchant marines against trespass. Of all the nations eager to pick up the shipping opportunities suddenly made available, young America was most ready and able.

The result was a rousing upsurge in the new nation's economy, which promptly rebounded from the war and the doldrums experienced during the 1770s and 1780s. Figure 1, showing the path of per-capita earnings from such items in the U.S. *balance of payments* as commodity exports and sales of shipping and mercantile services to foreigners before and during the period of conflict, graphically confirms this stimulus. Clearly, the values of commodities and services exported rose dramatically, and as noted by Douglass North:

> There can be no doubt that the years 1793 through 1807 were extraordinarily prosperous for the American economy. The fact appears in the numerous literary descriptions by people who observed the economy during

1

that time and in the few figures we do have – such as urbanization increasing from 5 to 7.3 percent and rapid expansion of the major cities (Baltimore, Boston, New York, and Philadelphia) between 1790 and 1810. There can also be little doubt that the period between 1793 and 1808 was one of full employment, in which our resources were utilized completely. . . . With [Jefferson's] embargo, this prosperity came to an end, and the year 1808 was characterized by depression and unemployment that reached the seacoast and the market-oriented sectors of the American economy.[1]

Great fortunes were built from commercial activities during this boom period, especially in New England and the middle Atlantic region. The capital accumulations of such famed entrepreneurs as John Jacob Astor, Archibald Gracie, Stephen Girard, E. H. Derby, and others vitalized the first stirrings of *industrialization* in North America and further enlarged an already developing *commercial sector*. Consequently, the strong commercial base was important not only because

Figure 1. Per-capita credits in balance of payments, 1790–1815. *Source:* Douglass C. North, "Early National Income Estimates of the U.S.," *Economic Development and Cultural Change*, IX, 3 (April 1961), p. 390.

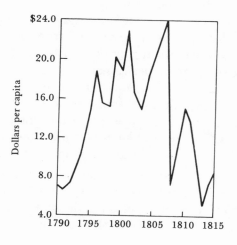

it gave the young United States the opportunity to capitalize on the prosperous trade conditions created by the Napoleonic Wars, but also for the longer-run effects. Commerce provided essential capital, entrepreneurial talent, and know-how for this budding industrialization.

It is difficult to overemphasize the importance of the commercial sector and the fact that it was already well established by 1793, and indeed much earlier. The rising merchant class has long been recognized as having spearheaded the move for independence by the thirteen revolting colonies. In addition, when a foreign war opened up exceptional trade opportunities, this merchant group was ready and able to provide the ships, physical installations and know-how to permit the new nation to seize its advantage. Thus the economic success of the nineteenth century actually stemmed from roots stretching well back into the colonial period. It was precisely the prior development of a strong commercial base (an advantage noticeably absent in other colonial areas of the New World) that gave a springboard for economic advancement and permitted the United States to play the leading role as a neutral in a time of war. As a consequence, the leading ports of the United States, and not those of the Caribbean, Latin America, or elsewhere, emerged as the centers of trade in the western Atlantic.

The impact of events on U.S. shipping activity after 1793 was similarly startling, and U.S. shipping earnings bounded upward from the stimulus of the war years. Further information is given in Figure 2, which shows total exports from the United States, 1790–1815. It should be noted that although domestically produced exports grew significantly, especially as cotton production spread throughout the South in response to England's demand for raw cotton for her textile mills, yet *reexports* formed a major portion of the total. American ships increasingly carried tropical and subtropical commodities such as cocoa, coffee, pepper, sugar, and spices to Europe and, in return, distributed European manufactures to the rest of the world. Obviously, then, the dominance of American shipping and commercial activity in the Atlantic was not due to a lack of demand for goods from the Caribbean or Latin America or other areas, but rather to their inadequately developed commercial sectors.

The purpose of this study is to discover just how this uniquely successful development of a commercial sector was achieved. It proved to be the critical factor in early U.S. development and placed the American economy among the most advanced of the period. Indeed, available evidence on *wealth* suggests that on the eve of the American Revolution the colonial economy was truly advanced, by comparison not only with other economies of that time but even with those of many countries today. Shockingly enough, countries comprising almost two-thirds of today's world population have *average per-capita incomes* at levels below that achieved by an average American two hundred years ago.

The rise of American colonial commerce is more than a mere success story, however. It offers important insights into economic change and the process of economic advance. With these facts in mind, it may be helpful to summarize briefly the analytical framework of this book. This framework is derived from economic theory, but its outlines are

Figure 2. Value of exports and reexports from U.S., 1790–1815. *Source:* Douglass C. North, *The Economic Growth of the United States, 1790–1860* (Englewood Cliffs, N.J.: Prentice-Hall, Inc. 1961) p. 28.

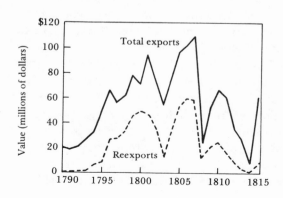

fundamentally bounded by the colonial experience and by the characteristics of an economy rich in land and in natural resources but facing drastic shortages of labor and capital. The analytical emphasis is based on a number of propositions regarding the effects of an expanding international economy on regional development.

Given the generally static nature of a rural frontier economy with a high degree of self-sufficiency by individuals and families, and with small and scattered domestic markets, any significant economic stimulation must depend upon the formation of external commercial ties. In the colonial case, the development of cash crops for export and the establishment of viable trade routes hastened *regional specialization.* In turn, the extension of overseas markets enlarged local market participation and money income and thus helped expand the domestic market. Accordingly, a greater degree of specialization, together with *division of labor,* also began to appear in such productive enterprises as family farms, plantations, stores, ships, and other businesses.

Recalling, then, that the hazards of frontier life generally impeded market exchange and made for greater concentration on self-sufficiency and nonmarket activities with low levels of *productivity,* we realize that many factors were at work in the expansion of the colonial economy. Population growth alone would reduce such hazards and thereby enhance market activity. Reductions in transportation costs played a critical role in expanding markets. Commercial linkages to other areas and among the colonies themselves stimulated commercial agriculture and aided productivity increases in that sector. Although rates of productivity advance were modest, such gains became self-perpetuating as self-sufficiency in *capital formation* further contributed to increases in labor productivity. Lastly, the process of learning-by-doing and of trial-and-error experimentation permitted successful adaptation of Old World skills and know-how to a hostile frontier environment.

These were the main forces in raising incomes above mere

subsistence levels and in propelling economic progress in the
colonies. Our emphasis here is on the continuing roles of the
market and of the rising resident commercial sector, for it
was this sector that provided the chief stimulus to market
expansion, economic specialization, capital accumulation,
and advancing productivity.

In short, commercial developments provided the leading
edge of colonial economic progress, and although more time
and effort were expended in many mundane economic activities, such as self-sufficient farming, hunting, woodcut-
ting, and the like, these were not critical to economic change.
Therefore, this study fails (by design) to illuminate all
corners of the colonial economy, and primary attention is
given to those activities and events that generated economic
growth and change.

We hope the lessons of the American colonial experience
will do more than pique scholarly interest. We believe they
have real possibilities for practical application and policy formation today in areas of the world that display those general
characteristics typical of the American colonial economy. In
these cases, it would appear that the most promising recom-
mendation would be for a policy of investment to increase
productivity in agriculture and to build a strong supportive
commercial sector – particularly the latter, because of its favorable spillover effects on other sectors.

Our story is that of the historical laying of such a commercial foundation, which resulted in greater achievement than
any other colonies in history have attained. To provide adequate perspective in this regard, we begin with Europe's first
outward reach to the New World.

Glossary of terms

Balance of payments
    A quantitative, accounting statement of the monetary value of all
    transactions between a nation and the rest of the world for a
    given period. The first section (the current account) represents

purchases and gifts of goods and services, and earnings and payments on foreign investments and all other income-affecting items. The second (the capital account) represents changes in indebtedness between a nation and the rest of the world. Credits in the balance of payments represent earnings of foreign exchange (foreign money), and debits represent payments to others (monetary outflows).

Industrialization

The growth of secondary types of production, most importantly manufacturing, as a proportion of total output.

Commercial sector

That part of economic activity devoted to producing commodities or services for sale in markets; as opposed to the subsistence sector, or the production of goods for one's own consumption. The typical colonist participated in both commercial and subsistence activities.

Reexports

Goods produced in a foreign area, imported from there, and then exported to another country.

Wealth

From the point of view of an individual economic entity, all property that has a monetary value because it is productive (i.e., contributes to the production of something economically valuable). From the point of view of society, wealth is all physical property (natural resources, including land, and capital goods) that is productive in the sense that it contributes to the production of goods and services.

Average income per person

Average per-capita income represents the monetary value of all goods and services produced by a society during a period of time, divided by the population of that society.

Regional specialization

Regional specialization in production results from differences in the opportunity to trade and from different conditions of production among areas. Each region will tend to produce and trade more of the items they can produce at lowest cost (relative to other regions).

Division of labor

Individual workers take on specialized tasks in production or distribution, instead of attempting to do everything necessary to produce or distribute a commodity or service.

Productivity

The relation between output of a good or service and the

amounts of inputs (labor, capital, and natural resources) needed to produce a given amount of output (output per unit of input).

Capital formation

Capital, or a capital good, is a physical factor of production used in the further production of other goods. It is a product itself of the economic system, such as a machine, a factory building, or a farm fence. The rate of capital formation is the pace at which an economy accumulates additional capital.

Selected readings

Bruchey, Stuart, *The Roots of American Economic Growth, 1607–1861: An Essay in Social Causation* (London: Hutchinson, 1965), Chapters 1, 2.

Dillard, Dudley, *Economic Development of the North Atlantic Community: Historical Introduction to Modern Economics* (Englewood Cliffs, N.J.: Prentice-Hall, 1967), Chapters 1–12.

North, Douglass C., *Growth and Welfare in the American Past: A New Economic History*, 2nd ed. (Englewood Cliffs, N.J.: Prentice-Hall, 1974), Chapter 4.

Shepherd, James F., and Gary M. Walton, *Shipping, Maritime Trade, and the Economic Development of Colonial North America* (Cambridge: Cambridge University Press, 1972), Chapters 1, 2.

2

The age of discovery and treasure

A speck of land in a vast ocean caught the eye of a certain seafaring Genoese captain on an October day in 1492. After due deliberation, Christopher Columbus chose to name his small island foothold San Salvador, and thus began the known history of the New World.

Although centuries would prove the landmark proportions of that discovery, Columbus himself would probably have disclaimed any paramount importance for it in the context of his own times. When Ferdinand and Isabella of Spain received word of the unknown land to the west, the news did little more than stir excitement at court and encourage further expeditions. Especially in economic terms, the short-run effects of the discovery were not to cause or to generate an era of economic expansion in Europe; indeed, a boom already underway for several decades had been the reason for the venture itself.

From the standpoint of economics, then, European prosperity had been launched earlier, about midway into the fifteenth century. Variations among regions make it difficult to pinpoint any precise year, but its beginning probably coincided with a sharp upturn in population somewhere around 1460, in recovery from the effects of the Hundred Years' War and the Black Death that in 1348–9 had killed at least one-third of the inhabitants of Western Europe. The surge in population was accompanied by an upswing in economic activity and an increase in trade, both within Europe and between Europe and Asia and Africa.

Columbus's voyage, which followed rather than preceded this economic upturn, was simply one among many such discoveries of that period. As a whole, they represented the extension of Europe into the Atlantic: a progression of outward strides that by 1492 had already been underway for more than seven decades. This persistent expansion of the European sphere of influence, rather than any single event, determined the course of history and set the stage for the birth of a New World. An analysis of that progression and the forces underlying the changes that occurred is prerequisite to understanding the causes and effects of Europe's foothold in America.

The long-distance trades

On the eve of America's discovery the wealth and commerce of Europe centered in the seafaring coastal regions of the Mediterranean, most notably in the northern Italian city-states of Genoa and Venice. Their economic power, which had been felt for over two centuries, was based squarely on the long-distance trades between Asia and Europe. The Mediterranean was a magnet linking the three great overland routes from Asia to the markets of Europe. Because of their locational advantage, and aided by superior commercial skills and know-how, Italian traders were able to dominate most of the world's expanding trades for centuries.

In that early period of material awakening in Europe, land transportation costs were exorbitant, and no cheap water route had yet been discovered. Consequently, goods traded over long distances tended to be light, and of low bulk relative to their value. Most important of these were expensive manufactures, such as soft cottons and silks from India and China, and jewel-toned rugs from Persia. Generally, such Asian luxuries so far surpassed the quality of similar European wares that even items subject to damage in transit, such as glass from Damascus and porcelain from China, found their way to the markets of Europe. Another important element of the long-distance trade was spices: cloves, nutmeg, ginger, and cinnamon were eagerly sought by medieval cooks to redeem European diets from monotony, and pepper served not only for seasoning but as a meat preservative–an essential virtue in warm climates.

The total value of European imports from Asia widely exceeded the value of goods exported to that market. Europe produced few items that were in great demand in Asia, or ones that could bear the high costs of transport. Compared to Asian wares, European goods tended to be of low value relative to their weight or bulk. Such an imbalance between imports and exports (which by the fifteenth century had long been a fact of European economic life) resulted in a continual drain of gold and silver to Asia. Reinforcing this outflow were payments for the costly land-transport services that were supplied primarily by non-Europeans.

In addition to the upsurge in the long-distance routes, trade was burgeoning within Europe as well. Here, also, the rest of the Continent relied heavily on Italian merchants for their supplies, especially of Mediterranean goods; the late fifteenth century saw a brisk traffic in grain, salt, salted fish, and other bulk commodities such as cheese, wine, and oil. In short, the Mediterranean had become a bustling trade arena.

The Atlantic pioneer

A wave of new discoveries accompanied the rise of commerce and trade in the last half of the fifteenth century, as more navigators found courage and incentive to follow the leaders over the horizon. And who *were* the leaders? Surprisingly, they came from a country on the periphery of contemporary trade routes. Whereas today's ventures into outer space are launched only by the wealthiest nations, the explorations of that day were almost ignored by the great Italian city-states except for an occasional offhand loan to finance some expedition or settlement. Nor was Spain more than a latecomer in the discoveries; it is almost an accident of history that an Italian sailor in the employ of Spain happened to make the most crucial of all the landfalls. Of many motives luring early European adventurers into the Atlantic, the foremost was the hope of developing additional markets and of tapping the riches of the long-distance trade from Asia. But the Mediterranean states were already wealthy and comfortable astride the traditional routes; why should they seek out new paths?

Not so Portugal, for that little seafaring nation had already sent out a few tentative expeditions even before the fifteenth century. By the time Columbus set sail, Portugal could claim more than seven decades of discovery, including Madeira and the Canary Islands, the settling of the Azores, and daring ventures far south along the western cost of Africa. Thus credit for the major preliminary thrusts into the Atlantic must go not to Spain or Italy, but to Portugal.

As early as 1415 Portuguese ventures had been given firm and persistent backing by the influence, enthusiasm, and wealth of Prince Henry the Navigator, a younger son of the king of Portugal. This visionary and active prince led Portugal into a vibrant period of exploration between 1415 and 1450, which included the establishment of a naval arsenal at Sagres and repeated expeditions dispatched down along the African shores.

Each new probe into the Atlantic added to seafaring experience and to the stockpile of knowledge of the winds and currents. Because of prevailing contrary winds, Cape Bojador, which was not far (26° latitude) down the western side of Africa, long had been considered the southern limit to Atlantic voyages. This barrier was now finally hurdled by the development of a new type of ship, a rugged, lateen-rigged caravel that (unlike the old squarerigger) could tack into the teeth of the trade winds and that eventually enabled Bartholomeu Dias to reach the Cape of Good Hope in 1488. Except for a mutinous crew that forced him back, he probably would have reached India on that same voyage. That accomplishment, however, was left to Vasco da Gama, who

nine years later reached India by the African all-water route
and returned safely to Portugal.

Expressed as a *rate of return on the capital invested,* the profits earned by Vasco da Gama's voyage approached 6,000
percent. Certainly a lucrative trade! Yet it is just as certain
that the earliest Portuguese expeditions down the African
coast were not motivated entirely by the ambitions of merchants, or of the Crown, with an eye strictly to the potential
wealth of Asia. Although the early forays along the African
coast required subsidization, the period of such needed support was fairly short, and in 1443 a profitable cargo of slaves
reached Portugal from Arguian. By the mid-1450s nearly a
thousand slaves per year were brought back from Africa,
many of them going to the burgeoning sugar plantations
under development on the Atlantic islands of Madeira, the
Azores, and the Canaries. This trade grew to nearly 3,500
slaves per year by the end of the century, and the trade in
sugar also grew apace.

Perhaps because these newly established trades were flourishing so well, further exploratory expeditions ceased for
nearly two decades after Sierra Leone was reached in 1448.
In 1469–74, however, the royal family renewed its initiative
and explorations took the Portuguese around the bulge of
Africa to the Bight of Biafra. These ventures opened up the
richest of the African trades, those in gold, ivory, and mar-
quette pepper, the latter an inferior but tolerable substitute
for Indian pepper. The Portuguese establishment of a fort
at Elmina on the Gold Coast brought to realization one of
their main objectives – to tap the gold caravans of Moors plying the desert. Portuguese control and development of West
Africa were delayed by a costly war with Castile from 1475
to 1479, but at its conclusion Castile formally acknowledged
in the peace treaty that the area would be recognized as an
exclusively Portuguese sphere.

By virtue of both West African and Atlantic-island trades,
Portugal now controlled a rich trading realm, and after 1479
these trades were unchallenged by foreign encroachment for

nearly fifty years. As the cargoes of gold, pepper, ivory, slaves, and sugar swelled, however, it was inevitable that Portugal must become increasingly visible to the rest of Europe and that her abounding wealth and activity in European markets would draw envious glances toward the opportunities lying over the horizon.

Meantime, an important corollary to the Portuguese explorations was taking place in mid-century at the other end of the Mediterranean. War efforts by the Turks were threatening to sever European commercial contact with the Muslim world, as they throttled Genoese trade along the traditional routes. Merchants who had enjoyed a fat trade with the East now found some of their capital unemployed, the more so as Portugal by 1471 had begun siphoning off Guinea gold to an extent that damaged Genoa's trade with the North African Moorish states. For these reasons much Genoese capital began to flow west to help develop new sugar plantations in the Atlantic islands, first in Madeira and in the Canaries, and later in the tropical islands of Fernando Póo and São Tomé. Perhaps even more important than Italian capital in the choice of new ships and the development of the trades was the availability of Italian know-how, skills, and commercial organization, which were the most advanced of their time.

Italy played no role, however, in the ultimate achievement of Portuguese explorations: the discovery of an all-water route to India. Although potentially great, the gains from exploring sea routes to Asia had long been considered so unsure and speculative that both Portuguese and Italian mercantile interests had concentrated instead on the numerous new Atlantic trades. This preoccupation was altered in 1482 when King John II initiated a new phase of exploration and ultimately sent the Portuguese around the tip of Africa and into the Indian Ocean.

It is sometimes overlooked that Columbus might have shared in this important phase of Portuguese exploration. Italy's itinerant son had actively sought support from the

Portuguese royal family for a proposal to sail west to Japan. Crown advisers, who possessed a sound knowledge of world geography, argued (correctly), however, that Columbus's proposal significantly understated the distance westward from Europe to Japan. Two additional events conspired against Columbus at this time. The Crown had just received news that Bartholomeu Dias (1450?–1500) had reached the Cape in 1488; and important new information about the navigation and commerce of the Indian Ocean was being sent back by Pedro de Covilhão (1450?–1545?), who had traveled to India by land. Because this combination assured the king of an all-water eastern route, the speculative goal of Japan was rejected in favor of the more certain one, India, which da Gama (1469?–1524) achieved in 1497. A few years later, a second voyage to India, undertaken by Cabral (1460?–1526?), brought the Portuguese to the coast of Brazil; hence Portugal also discovered the New World eight years after Columbus and, similarly, quite by accident. Over-all, there can be little doubt that in the perspective of their day, da Gama, not Columbus, could claim credit for the more celebrated and rewarding discovery.

An all-water route to the Indian and Asian markets offered not only great economic opportunities, but great military possibilities as well, because vessels sailing the Indian Ocean were no match for the well-armed ships of Portugal now intruding in those waters. Taking full advantage of their prowess, the Portuguese freely used armed force to block the traditional flows of goods and to win trading concessions from rulers in the East. Indians, Arabs, and others who had been in control of these Asian trades had no arms to match the naval artillery brought from Europe by the Portuguese. Nevertheless, these excursions greatly strained tiny Portugal's resources in soldiers, seamen, and ships, and they drastically cut into the profits of the eastern trade. Moreover, despite such disruptions, trade persisted along the traditional routes. The preeminence of Venice in the eastern trade was not destroyed until after 1600, when the

Dutch East India Company accomplished the coup by economic means: superior efficiency in shipping and in commercial organization.

The rise of the Atlantic economies

Although Portugal had failed to block the flow of goods over traditional land routes, commerce was expanding in the Atlantic to a degree that ultimately remapped the economic landscape of Europe. Growth of the sugar and slave trades resulted in the settlement and development of the Atlantic islands, and the bountiful trade with West Africa has already been emphasized. By the turn of the century, many European docksides were receiving spices via the all-water route. Portugal virtually controlled this trade, the exceptions being some Spanish influence in the Canaries and the insertion of some Italian capital transfers or loans, chiefly from Genoa.

As these South Atlantic trades developed, the relative economic position of the Mediterranean began to slip back. Its absolute volume of trade continued at a healthy increase in the sixteenth century, but not in proportion to the Atlantic trades. The centers of commerce and wealth, and the balance of power, were shifting steadily to the nations bordering the Atlantic.

At the same time that Portugal's discoveries and colorful seafaring ventures were initiating new southern and eastern trades, other developments to the north were reinforcing the change in patterns of European commerce. Cabot's expedition from England led to the discovery of Newfoundland in 1497 and spurred fishing activity in the north, but of even greater consequence was the expansion of commerce in the older established trades of northern Europe. Trade in the hardy temperate-zone products of grain, salt, salted fish, woolen cloth, furs, iron, timber, and naval stores grew disproportionately. These were not luxury items, like those from Asia; but because they were transported almost entirely by sea, these items of high weight or bulk relative to their value could bear these relatively low costs. Moreover, the Atlantic fringe areas were well positioned and experienced to supply more than seafaring services.

By the turn of the century, certain parts of Europe were becoming densely populated: more farmers were plowing fewer acres per farm – or acres of poorer quality. Though more crops were being harvested, the growth of output was falling below the ever-expanding demand for food: such areas as Spain, Portugal, and certain industrializing regions of the Low Countries could no longer supply their own needs, but came to rely heavily on imports from France and the Baltic. Coincidentally, the need for more ships was putting pressure on the supplies of timber and naval stores along the Baltic. French salt and wine were shipped into that region as well as to England and Holland, and Holland shipped herring both north and south. The most important manufactured item was woolen cloth, for which major centers developed in eastern England, northern France, Flanders, and Holland, as well as in northern Italy.

The upsurge of trade through the Baltic is suggested by the bare fact that the number of vessels annually plying that sea increased from about 1,300 early in the sixteenth century to approximately 5,000 near its close; but even this understates the rise in trade, since the size of the vessels was steadily growing as well.

The northern European trades differed in another important way from the luxury trades to Asia: the ratio of inbound to outbound cargo was quite different. On any outward voyage to India or the East Indies, the ships were relatively empty, while in the northern trades ships holds were filled for both legs of the journey. Such capacity utilization, of course, aided trade by keeping down average freight costs per ton shipped.

Development of these and other trades ultimately led to the dazzling preeminence of early-sixteenth-century Antwerp as an *entrepôt* for the city-states of northern Italy, and the trade centers of Germany, England, and Holland. This city's prosperity was founded on the distribution of German wares of silver, copper, lead, and zinc, and of Italian, Flemish, and English manufactures; but these trades were so brisk that they attracted to Antwerp the auxiliary financial, shipping, and commercial services that were required as well. The city became a magnet, pulling in merchants from all over Europe to settle into permanent colonies, which lent Antwerp an unmatched cosmopolitan atmosphere. There the English found both ready markets for their woolens and linens and a source of German and Baltic wares. The Portuguese sold African pepper and Madeira sugar, plus Asian spices, while obtaining German copper and copperware for the African trade and silver for their Asian exchanges.

The rise of Antwerp was inseparably linked to the rise of the Atlantic trades, and the growth of this particular city is explained by its advantageous location. *Aggregate demand* was increased by a number of factors, especially the expansion of population and growing *urbanization*. Supply factors were also at work. For instance, it became easier and less risky to negotiate market exchanges; insurance coverage became more common, which further reduced risks in long-distance trades. In addition, as noted above, there were important improvements in shipping and navigation during this period.

That particular seaboard corner was further benefited when new discoveries of copper, lead, zinc, and silver deposits in southern Germany, Hungary, and Poland stimulated demand throughout Western Europe and the Mediterranean. Like the Italian city-states at an earlier date, Antwerp now sat astride the great crossroads of trade, holding the reins of commerce between the regions of the Baltic, the British Isles, the south Atlantic, Germany, the Mediterranean, and the Lowlands. By the late fifteenth century, the Netherlands as a region had become one of the most densely populated and economically advanced areas in Europe, and the center of many small luxury industries such as sugar refining, paper production and printing, jewelry, and the dyeing and finishing of English woolens.

Antwerp's zenith was reached around 1560, when it boasted a population in excess of 100,000, matched or surpassed in the West only by Paris, London, and Seville. Trading activity for all practical purposes was continuous throughout the year, although four lengthy and opulent fair times annually served as periods of financial settlement. War and the division of the Netherlands between 1572 and 1585 precipitated the end of Antwerp's supremacy. However, the city's decline had begun by the mid-1560s. The prosperity of Central Europe had begun to weaken prior to that time, sapped by the peasant wars of 1526 and a series of religious and dynastic struggles that disrupted production and trade. Moreover, the silver mines of Central Europe were cutting back their production, since the value of silver was decreasing.

At this point, perhaps for the first time, the treasures of the New World had become a truly critical factor in shaping the economics of Europe. For it was the influx of American silver pouring in from far shores that undercut silver production in Europe. Moreover, the overflowing coffers of Spanish-American silver at Cadiz now offered an attractive alternative entrepôt to the Portuguese Indies trade. Most important of all, however, the flow of silver from America, which grew to remarkable heights by the last half of the century, provided the sinews of war and whetted the Spanish Crown's appetite for empire.

Clearly the voyages of discovery, together with the swelling tides of commerce, were now exerting heavy pressure on the economic structure and balance of power in Europe. Dramatic shifts had occurred by the late sixteenth century, and the slight short-run effects of the discoveries were giving way to their highly significant long-run effects, especially in the case of Columbus. Contemporary Europeans had lightly dismissed his discovery as minor. Later observers were beginning to understand what we now realize: that he had led Spain to the threshold of riches and an empire that won the envy of Europe.

American mines and European prices

For more than a decade after Columbus's discovery, Spanish, Portuguese, French, and English expeditions continued the search for a western ,passage to the East. The length and breadth of the New World soon became apparent, however, and gradually newly recognized opportunities in America began to divert the attention of these fortune seekers. As the most vigorous explorers in the New World, the Spanish conquistadores handed over to the Crown dominion over most of America. Only Portugal's claim to Brazil prevented Spain's complete and total dominance of the new continent; and only their presence, plus occasional intrusions by French and English traders in American waters, disturbed that situation until near the end of the sixteenth century.

Unlike his first transatlantic crossing, Columbus's subsequent voyages received only encouragement from the Crown. The more substantive financial support for ships and stores was supplied for the most part by Spanish nobles and merchants who willingly risked their ,investments on a profitable return cargo or on a lucrative claim in America. This early source of investment soon became uncommon, however. By 1506 a few Spanish colonists had accumulated sizable fortunes from gold found on the island of Hispaniola. Some reinvested their profits in exploration and settlement in Cuba, Jamaica, and Puerto Rico, and this pattern of financing continued as Spain stepped from one foothold to the next. True, capital from Spain had financed the first settlements on the mainland; but it was profits from investments in Cuba that backed the series of mainland expeditions after 1516 and that led to the conquest of Mexico by Cortes. In turn, the following decade of explorations and conquests throughout the New World was financed by wealth extracted from Mexico.

Actually, it was only in the first decade or two after Columbus's discovery that the motherland of Spain made significant net investment in America. National expenditures continued for a time on ships to be used in trade and for defense, but increasingly these and other investments in the New World were derived from retained profits on previous American ventures. By mid-century the investment process had definitively reversed itself, with net capital flows steadily going from America to Spain. Overall, then, Spain's empire in America rested for the most part on wealth acquired and reinvested there.[1]

Although Spanish intervention in the New World had a dramatic impact on the lives of native Americans, it also had profound repercussions in Europe. Although the underlying statistics are not without question, Figure 3 illustrates the flow of gold and silver from America to Europe. The lion's share of these Spanish imports, those in silver, came after 1560, and in total they tripled the total *supply of money* in Europe over its level at the beginning of the century.

These inflows of precious bullion won the envy of other nations, stimulated trade throughout Europe, helped remap the economic contours of sixteenth-century Europe, and initiated a period of prolonged price rise that in terms of gold

Figure 3. Spanish imports of American treasure. *Source:* Earl J. Hamilton, *American Treasure and the Price Revolution in Spain, 1501–1650* (Cambridge, Mass.: Harvard University Press, 1934), p. 34.

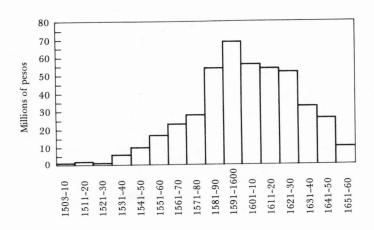

and silver is without parallel. Fires of *inflation* steadily height-
ened throughout Europe, carrying Spanish prices in 1600 to
340 percent of their level in 1500; England experienced a
rise of 260 percent in the century, and France 220 percent.

A pioneering study by Earl J. Hamilton, *The Price Revolution in Europe,* was the forerunner of serious scrutiny by
many economic historians of this phenomenal impact of
American treasure on European prices, commerce, and economic growth. Hamilton's argument about the effects of
these inflows of treasure upon European economic growth is
summarized in his 1952 address as president of the Economic History Association:

> It is difficult . . . to see how anything else could have
> been more important than the great lag of wages behind
> prices in certain economically advanced countries dur-
> ing the Price Revolution. Capitalism required *capital,*
> and it would not be easy to imagine a more powerful
> instrument for providing it than forced saving through
> a highly favorable price-wage ratio. The high rates of
> profit when prices were rising and wages, the chief cost,
> were lagging gave a strong inducement to invest savings
> in productive enterprises. Rising prices penalized delay
> in investment and by lowering the effective rate of inter-
> est encouraged borrowing for investment in anticipation
> of earnings. In short, rising prices and lagging wages
> provided capital and gave strong incentives to use it
> capitalistically. Other things anywhere near equal, capi-
> talism could hardly have failed to flourish.[2]

Alternatively stated, Hamilton contends that although the
influx of American treasure tended to drive up both prices
and wages, the fact that prices initially far outpaced wages
altered the *distribution of income and wealth* in favor of the
merchant and capitalist classes, thus favoring those with unusually strong inclinations to save and invest. This in turn
led to higher rates of capital formation and of *economic
growth* in Europe. How true is this assertion?

To a limited extent the evidence does support Hamilton's position, and prices did rise relative to wages throughout Europe. In other words, *real wages* (what money wages could buy in terms of actual commodities) were declining. A graphical illustration of this decline, 1500–1600, is given in Figure 4 for Spain, England, and France; and data on wage and price movements for a longer period in England and France are shown in Tables 1 and 2.

Although there are limits to the usefulness of these statistics, it is broadly clear that both prices and wages increased; these trends are consistent with the large influx of precious metals noted in Figure 3. Tables 1 and 2 show, however, that the upward march of prices relative to wages did not favor

Figure 4. Indices of real wages during the sixteenth century for England, Spain, and France. *Source:* E. H. Phelps Brown and S. V. Hopkins, "Builders' Wage-Rates, Prices and Population: Some Further Evidence" *Economica*, XXVI (1959), pp. 18–38; adapted from D.C. North and R.P. Thomas, *The Rise of the Western World: A New Economic History* (Cambridge: Cambridge University Press, 1973), p. 111.

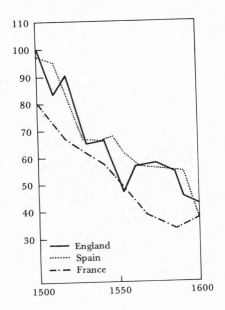

Table 1. Price and wage trends in England, 1500–1702 (1451–1500 = 100)

	1521–30	1551–60	1583–92	1613–22	1643–52	1673–82	1693–1702
Wiebe's price index[a]	113	132	198	257	331	348	339
Unprocessed agricultural products[b]	132	179	262	402	478	466	518
Assorted industrial products[c]	110	116	150	176	217	200	239
Wood and wood products[d]	87	119	185	259	300	420	395
Imported food products[e]	151	119	146	124	151	–	163
Wiebe's wage index	93	88	125	134	175	205	233

[a]Georg Wiebe, *Zur Geschichte der Preisrevolution des XVI und XVII Jahrhunderts* (Leipzig, 1895), pp. 374–7. Wiebe's price and wage series, compiled from price and wage data in J. E. Thorold Rogers, *A History of Agriculture and Prices in England* (Oxford, 1887), IV and V, consist of a simple arithmetic average of 79 price relatives computed decennially, and a similarly computed average of 8 wage relatives.

[b]Average of price relatives of the following commodities: wheat, barley, oats, peas, beans, malt, oxen, pigs, lambs, hens, geese. These are the raw food products for which price relatives are given for all or most of the 200-year period.

[c]The components are lime, salt, wrought iron, pewter, slate, gutter tiles, paper, shirting, canvas, and cloth. These are manufactured items for which price relatives are given for all or most of the 200-year period.

[d]Firewood, laths, charcoal.

[e]Sugar, cinnamon, raisins, pepper, nutmeg, cloves.

Source: David Felix, "Profit Inflation and Industrial Growth: The Historic Record and Contemporary Analogies," *Quarterly Journal of Economics*, LXX (August 1956), p. 446.

Table 2. *Price and wage trends in France, 1500–1700 (1451–1500 = 100)*

	1501–25	1526–50	1551–75	1576–1600	1601–25	1626–50	1651–75	1676–1700
Wiebe's price index[a]	113	136	174	248	189	243	227	229
Selected agricultural index[b]	136	163	250	429	259	402	345	315
Index of assorted manufactures[c]	96	130	122	144	129	143	133	161
Wiebe's wage index	92	104	103	113	113	127	127	125

[a]Wiebe, op. cit., pp. 378–9. Wiebe's price index is a simple 25-year average of 39 price relatives, based on the compilations of Comte d'Avenal.

[b]Rye, wheat, vegetables, meat, eggs, milk.

[c]Iron, lead, copper, footwear, linen, clothing, cloth (2 grades).

Source: See Table 1.

industrial or manufactured goods. Hamilton's analysis was incomplete and at too aggregate a level to reveal that the main factor in the rise of the general price index was the soaring prices of food and of those goods related to agriculture. Moreover, the prices of finished goods rose less than the prices of their raw-material components. Thus the overall evidence strongly suggests that the redistribution of wealth was not so much from laborer to capitalist, but rather from the nonagricultural to the agricultural sector.

Such redistribution of income between sectors is consistent with the historical record on population growth and changes in agriculture. The rapid increase of population during this period led to extremes of *diminishing returns* in agriculture, such that further additions of labor and capital to the land brought about very small additions of output. Therefore, as land became relatively scarce and labor-land ratios increased, average as well as marginal returns to labor effort fell to very low levels. The comparatively large increases in population and the supply of labor tended to hold wages down. At the same time, supplies of agricultural products were not advancing in proportion to demand because of extremely *low marginal returns to labor* in agriculture; thus agricultural prices rose relative to other goods. For this same reason, rents on land soared faster and higher than did commodity prices. Landowners, not merchants or industrial capitalists, stood to gain most from the relative price movements of that period.

It is also important to distinguish between *relative and absolute price changes.* The influx of treasure in combination with other changes in the money supply did indeed cause inflation: all prices rose in absolute amounts. But this fails to consider the change in relative prices. Why did certain prices move upward less drastically than other prices, or wages compared to rents? For these differential movements, as noted above, information is needed on the conditions of supply and demand for various goods and productive resources and on how these conditions changed over the period. The force that spurred inflation generally cannot explain such differences in price movements.

The same specie flows that produced this general inflation on the Continent proved eventually to be a well-disguised curse to their originator. In an era when wealth and power were inseparable, Spain was riding the crest of the silver tide. In a unique position, she could afford to pay cash for goods from other countries without having to produce exports in return. As a result, Spain failed to build a productive economic base to support its political dominion. In addition, the overflowing national treasure chest apparently offered an irresistible temptation to arm more troops and to reach out for more power. Spain's frequent forays in the latter part of the sixteenth century, culminating in the defeat of the Spanish Armada in 1588, signaled the undoing of a great empire and the ebbing of Spanish power throughout Europe.

In combination, Spanish funds paid out for imports, and as military pay to soldiers on foreign soil, led to the redistribution of American treasure throughout Europe. Of course, some of this treasure was reexported to Asia, but that which remained helped to monetize the economies of Europe and to facilitate increased exchanges in regional and international trade. The rise of money relative to commodity production also may have helped pull productive resources out of subsistence activities and into more specialized activities associated with market exchange. In this respect New World treasure was a positive force that added to the economic vitality of that period.

Nevertheless, its role has undoubtedly been exaggerated,[3] and the presence of American wealth did not of its own cause a redistribution of income that led to growth. Indeed, the impact of a downward spiral to very low marginal returns to labor in agriculture and the accompanying fall in real wages caused a decline in well-being for many workers; perhaps there was no growth in real per-capita incomes throughout much of the period. The rise of commerce, trade, and income were apparent—but not necessarily in advance of the increase in population, especially in the latter half of the sixteenth century. For this period, the growth of per-capita income that Hamilton attempted to explain may in fact merely be illusory, and overall, the various components of the Hamilton thesis are not supported by the evidence.

However, Europe's economic problems did not stop its outward reach. Indeed, one of the most important long-run effects of the New World discovery was the relief it offered to land-hungry, overcrowded citizens of the Old World. Those who dared, might find land overseas in undreamed-of expanses. However, this was a long-range solution that required settlement and colonization, and it did not materialize significantly until the seventeenth century, when the French and the English proved the most active and successful forerunners in this great adventure.

The English settlements, in particular, led to a growth of trade in commodities—raw materials from America in exchange for European manufactures—that laid the foundation of a new empire. Unlike the linkage of its American empire to Spain, which largely represented a one-way siphoning-off of resources, the permanent settlements from England forged a viable two-way economic bond too strong to be broken by the exhaustion of veins of ore.

Glossary of terms

Rate of return on capital

  The earnings (or contribution to output) due to a particular capital good or group of capital goods, as a percentage of its (their) cost.

Entrepôt

  Literally, a warehouse, but commonly used to refer to a main center for trade and commercial activity, such as London in the eighteenth century, or New York today.

Aggregate demand

  The monetary value of all final goods and services, capital goods, and governmental services that all economic units (consumers, businesses, governments, and foreigners) are willing to purchase during a period of time, such as a year. The amount demanded is positively related to income.

Urbanization

This occurs over time when a growing proportion of a total population comes to live in towns and cities (urban centers).

Inflation

A rise in the general or average level of prices for goods and services; or equivalently, a decrease in the purchasing power of a unit of money.

Distribution of income and wealth

Income for society is the stream of earnings from economic activity; or, equivalently, the value of output of goods and services produced during a given period of time. Wealth is property that has economic value (a "stock" compared with a "flow" of income). The distribution of income and wealth refers to the particular division of income and wealth among individuals or various groups in society.

Economic growth

Economic growth occurs when material standards of living increase over time. A sustained increase in real per-capita income or output is usually taken as an indication, and sometimes a measure, of economic growth.

Real wage

A real wage is the money wage adjusted for changes in the purchasing power of money.

Diminishing returns in agriculture

Diminishing returns in agriculture refer to the decreasing additional output of agricultural goods obtained as more variable inputs of labor and capital are added to agricultural production on a fixed or given land area.

Low marginal returns to labor in agriculture

Low marginal returns to labor in agriculture refer to a situation where little additional agriculture output is obtained as additional amounts of labor are used in agricultural production.

Absolute price change

An absolute price change is the amount by which the price of any good or service changes.

Relative price change

A relative price change is the amount by which the price of a good or service changes with respect to the prices of other goods and services.

Selected readings

Cipolla, Carlo M., *Before the Industrial Revolution: European Society and Economy, 1000–1700* (New York: W. W. Norton, 1976), Chapters 5–10.

Davis, Ralph, *The Rise of the Atlantic Economies* (Ithaca, N.Y.: Cornell University Press, 1973), Chapters 1, 2.

Doughty, Robert A., "Industrial Prices and Inflation in Southern England, 1401–1640," *Explorations in Economic History*, XII, 2 (April 1975), pp. 177–92.

Felix, David, "Profit Inflation and Industrial Growth: The Historic Record and Contemporary Analogies," *Quarterly Journal of Economics*, LXX (August 1956), pp. 441–63.

Hamilton, Earl J., *American Treasure and the Price Revolution in Spain, 1501–1650* (Cambridge, Mass.: Harvard University Press, 1934).

– "American Treasure and the Rise of Capitalism (1500–1700)," *Economica*, IX (November 1929), pp. 338–57.

– "Prices as a Factor in Business Growth," *Journal of Economic History*, XII, 4 (Fall 1952), pp. 325–49.

Nef, John U., "Prices and Industrial Capitalism in France and England, 1540–1640," *Economic History Review*, VII (May 1937), pp. 155–85.

North, Douglass C., and Robert P. Thomas, *The Rise of the Western World* (Cambridge: Cambridge University Press, 1973), Chapter 9.

3

Taking the frontier

Spain reaches first

There is an old saying that "the Quakers came to America to do good and ended up doing well." Such a quip emphasizes equally well the dual motives of other early settlers in America, most notably perhaps the Spanish, who were the first to secure a foothold in the New World. For the Spanish primarily colonized America for the joint purpose of christianizing the native Indians and extracting the New World's wealth.

To accomplish this double objective the Spanish introduced a practice called *encomienda* (commendation), which they had developed earlier in the Canary Islands shortly after their takeover there. To convert the Indians to Christianity and to "civilize" the indigenous population, each village was placed under the "protection and authority" of a Spanish overseer. For his services and direction, the overseer was entitled to labor from the villagers and to tribute from them in gold, silver, or commodities. The immediate responsibility for the day-to-day direction of encomienda, of course, rested with the Spanish overseers, who were little influenced in any practical way by the remote Crown or Church from whom ultimately they derived their authority. Consequently many persons abused the system for the sake of personal enrichment by extracting exorbitant amounts of labor in a fashion not unlike prison gang labor.

In the first several decades of Spanish control, which was concentrated in the islands of the Caribbean, this system proved especially harsh. In many respects it was actually worse than slavery, because the overseers did not hold *property rights* in the natives themselves. Therefore they had little incentive to care for them properly. They did have claim to their labor services, however, which instilled incentives to work the Indians relentlessly. The effects of overwork and the spread of European diseases, mainly smallpox, measles, and typhus, virtually wiped out the island populations. For instance, within several decades the native population of Hispaniola fell from approximately 300,000 to several hundred. The populations of Cuba and Puerto Rico suffered similar fates, and although Spain did not actually settle the Bahamas and some of the Leeward islands, their populations were raided and stripped to work the mines of Puerto Rico.

The futility and immorality of this system did not go undetected, but encomienda proved difficult to eliminate. After all, it was profitable to the overseer in the short run, and it offered strong encouragement to Spanish citizens to migrate to the New World. Nevertheless, the excesses experienced on the islands were gradually curbed on the mainland, and in 1549 encomienda was outlawed, although elements of the system lingered thereafter.

Despite stricter controls over local overseers and other improvements, harsh treatment and disease continued to take its toll of the native population. Within two decades of Cortes's conquest of Mexico in 1519–21 the preconquest population of 25 million had been cut in half. This decline continued throughout Spanish America; from a population in 1500 that probably was close to that of Europe's, it had slid by 1600 to only one-tenth that of Europe. Consequently, while some may wish to emphasize the gift of Christianity—in exchange for bullion–Spain's main impact on early America was the destruction of the native people.

The flow of Spanish settlers to the New World only partially offset the losses of the indigenous population, and the Spaniards in the New World remained a small minority. By 1574 the Spanish population in Spanish America was approximately 160,000. Even by 1650 there were only about a half million who were white or predominantly white. Most of these were males of working age and Spanish born, since few women and children were attracted to the New World. In addition there were about a half million black slaves from Africa who worked the sugar islands in the Caribbean plus another half million people of mixed blood. By the mid-seventeenth century there were little more than 2 million "pure" Indians in all of Spanish America including Mexico and the central regions of Peru and Bolivia.

In addition to these striking changes in the population, there were important cultural and organizational changes in the daily lives of the people. Besides the obvious impact of Christian training and the mischief of encomienda, new European techniques, commodities, and animals altered economic activity in America. Although Spanish attention focused mainly on the mining of precious metals, the basic structure of the economy remained agrarian. But that agrarian life was radically influenced by the introduction and spread of European crops, including wheat, barley, rye, and sugar, onions, cabbage, peas, and apples and peaches. In addition, inasmuch as the llama, the dog, and the turkey constituted the whole of the indigenous livestock, the arrival of horses, cows, oxen, hogs, chickens, and sheep led not only to herding activities and improved diets, but also to lower land transportation costs and heavy plowing. And of course the introduction of metallurgy and guns and gunpowder also had significant effects.

Many items previously unknown to Europe, such as tobacco, corn, beans, peanuts, potatoes, pumpkins, squash, tomatoes, avocados, chocolate, and vanilla, remained important crops in Spanish America, but these did not form a basis of commercial agriculture. Sugar was the only cash crop of any importance in transatlantic trade, and it was more than a century after Columbus before sugar production was developed in the New World. As noted, throughout the sixteenth century the native populations on the Caribbean islands dwindled. So too did the Spanish populations there. By the mid-seventeenth century, the islands were crowded with African slaves working Spanish-run sugar plantations.

It is important to recognize the impact of sugar cultivation on the pattern of Spanish settlement. In contrast to the typical pattern of treasure extraction by forced labor, the sugar plantations were developed for the purpose of production for export. Forced labor continued to characterize Spanish enterprise, but the plantations marked an important departure from the usual features of Spanish (impermanent) settlement. As the sugar plantations developed and Spanish migrants and African slaves poured in, Spanish settlement took on deeper roots and became more permanent. It initiated agrarian capitalism in the New World.

Impermanent "nonsettlement" characteristics of Spanish colonization emphasizing extraction also typically characterized the early activities of the Dutch, French, and British in North America. However, the failure to locate high-valued mineral deposits forced these latecomers into other endeavors, most notably the extraction of furs and fish. Of the three, the French were perhaps the most adept at encouraging the native Indians to trap and exchange furs, but in general the more elusive North American Indian was not exploited like his southern brethren. Consequently the pervasive aspect of extraction by forced native labor was less prevalent in North America.

Although most of the early French, Dutch, and British ventures took the form of either temporary fishing bases or trading stations (mainly for furs), the first British outpost was actually a base for privateering (a euphemism for piracy). This "settlement" was established in the Carolinas in the 1580s by Sir Walter Raleigh to harass Spanish treasure fleets. This first British settlement, known as the Roanoke colony, stands as one of history's fascinating mysteries. It disappeared without a trace around 1590. No one from this "lost colony" was ever found and no records were left.

The British foothold

The Roanoke experience forcefully underlines the great hardships faced by new settlers in North America. In fact, a majority of the earliest settlers died within two years of their arrival, either from disease, starvation, Indian attack, or some other source. Obviously, few people were willing to face such perils and migration to the new world was not a routine experience. Moreover, the costs of ocean passage in the early seventeenth century were extremely high – close to £10 per person, which probably exceeded a full year's income for an average Englishman at that time.

Despite the high costs, the anticipated gains from colonization were sufficient to attract both capital and labor. The institutional form initially used to spearhead English settlement and to organize and to direct that capital and labor was the joint stock company. Many such companies had been chartered during Elizabeth's reign, for the purpose of developing trading spheres, mainly in Asia. For instance, the Muscovy Company was chartered in 1555 to find a northeast passage (through Russia) to Asia, the African Company was chartered in 1588 to develop the slave trade, the Levant Company was initiated in 1592 to trade throughout the Mediterranean, and the East India Company was established in 1602 to develop the all-water route to Asia.

These companies, giant enterprises in their time, typically enjoyed exclusive rights to their particular trading realms. In fact it was a common practice for the Crown to grant monopolylike privileges, where these might strengthen the empire. Rather than as a restriction on trade, which is the way we commonly view monopolistic behavior today, these early monopolies often acted to create markets and expand trade. Monopoly privileges provided an important incentive to overseas investment, especially in the trades to Asia and elsewhere. These long-distance trades were extremely risky and typically required substantial investments in the form of "start-up" costs. Such costs were necessary to establish trading stations and to develop trading contracts, often by way of bribes and payoffs to local chieftains and officials. Exclusive monopoly rights prevented undesired competitive bidding (from the viewpoint of the Crown and the empire) for these contracts and assured the first company or trader that a later arrival would not take advantage of their initial efforts and participate in trade at their expense. Therefore when these conditions prevailed the Crown often permitted monopoly practices to go on in place of competitive efforts.

Of course the Crown had an important stake in colonization and endeavored to encourage these new trades. In this era of *mercantilism* and empire building, colonies were important for their strategic location and as sources of raw materials. Colonization was encouraged to make the mother country less dependent on other nations for important products and in general to foster greater economic self-sufficiency, which was especially important during wartime. As a matter of mercantilist policy, colonies were valued most when they helped reduce the outflow of bullion to other countries. Consequently colonies were highly valued when they produced items that obviated the need for imports from rival countries. Such import substitutions curbed the outflow of gold and silver and increased economic interdependence. Undoubtedly, it was the hope of every investor in North America that the Spanish experience with rich treasure discoveries might be duplicated. But it was more the buoyant fur market in England, especially for beaver fur (for hats), that helped to encourage the formation of many of the earliest British trading companies in North America. A host of new companies was established in the early seventeenth century, including the London Company (later renamed the Virginia Company), the New Plymouth Company, the Massachusetts Bay Company, the Providence Islands (Carolinas) Company, the New Foundland Company, and others. These were modeled after the great eastern trading companies and to a large extent were funded from fortunes earned in those older trades. These institutions can take credit for establishing the first permanent British settlements on the frontier, but their success was limited to securing a colonial foothold. In terms of costs and revenues these ventures were notorious financial failures.

The North American ventures discovered no gold or silver mines or populous ancient civilizations ready to exchange exotic wares, such as tea, silk, and spices, for European commodities. Unlike the Asian trades, North America offered no quick riches. Consequently, the relatively successful trading-post establishments, characteristic of Spanish America and the Far East, proved inadequate for the more demanding tasks required for settlement in North America. This new frontier required a different and more permanent form of settlement.

The hard lessons of frontier hazards proved painful to settlers and investors alike. The first settlement to take hold permanently was the Jamestown colony, established by the London Company in 1607. In that year three tiny vessels, four months out of London and carrying 105 people, moored in Chesapeake Bay. For the most part these people were more adventurers than settlers, and they were easily distracted by futile searches for treasure and other get-rich-quick schemes. For instance, they sent shiploads of mica and yellow ore to England in 1607 and 1608 only to disappoint everyone who had hoped that this worthless cargo might be gold. Despite provisions from the ships, and what could be produced from the land and the forests, disease, starvation, and misadventure killed 67 of the original 105 within the first year.[1]

In 1609 the remaining group was joined by 800 new settlers sent by the reorganized and renamed Virginia Company. But by the spring of the next year, frontier hardships had reduced their number to 60. That same summer, these survivors were en route downriver to return to England when three shiploads of supplies and new settlers met and encouraged them to change their plans. It must have been a difficult decision for, as Charles Andrews put it:

This was the "Starving Time" for Virginia, just as there
were to be starving times for Bermuda, Plymouth, and
Barbados, when men suffered and died, because they
had not yet learned the art of colonization, and had
come to America inadequately supplied and equipped
and unfamiliar with the method of wresting a living
from the wilderness.[2]

Despite support from the company, Jamestown continued
to languish. The major problem was the failure to discover
a cash crop that would make a commercial success of the
settlement. As noted above, like other nations Britain was
straining to improve its balance of payments and to increase its inward flow of gold and silver. Over the years the
Crown encouraged a host of schemes in the colonies for the
purpose of *import substitution,* including the production of
wine, glass, and silk. But each of these particular instances
suffered misadventure. On other occasions, however, the
trial-and-error approach succeeded. The most important
case, especially for the Chesapeake region, was when tobacco plants were introduced at Jamestown by John Rolfe a
few years after its founding. The soil and climate were
found to be ideal for tobacco cultivation, and English tastes
for tobacco were being whetted, despite efforts by King
James I to discourage his subjects from engaging in "so vile
and stinking a custom." Sir Walter Raleigh had popularized
the use of tobacco and in spite of the king England was
then importing more than £200,000 of tobacco annually
from Spain. By 1620 the desire to shut off this drain of
specie to Spain surpassed the Crown's reluctance to tolerate
this "stinking custom." After proven successes of production in Virginia the Privy Council granted the Virginia
Company exclusive rights to the English market, banned all
English production, and guaranteed to ban it elsewhere
within the Empire. In return it required that all Virginia
tobacco be sold exclusively in England. Suddenly, tobacco
became the Virginia *staple* and within two years of its intro-

duction £100,000 of tobacco was shipped to England from Virginia.

In addition to the vital introduction of tobacco, the James-town colony and the Virginia Company undertook many organizational changes important to production efficiency. Operating originally as a collective, the colony fared poorly because of disincentives to work and to innovate. The initial collective methods of production and shared consumption failed because they created discontent, and encouraged indi-viduals to shirk assigned tasks. Single men complained of working for other men's wives and children without recom-pense, and the strong thought it an injustice that they re-ceive no more in clothes and victuals than persons capable of only half the work. Similarly, women viewed working for men other than their husbands as a type of slavery. Because land was owned in common incentives to work it were want-ing. However, as private holdings came to replace those held in common, work attitudes improved as individuals came to expect the full return for their efforts, rather than to share their output and improvements with others. The first step toward private property was in 1614, with limits of three-acre holdings; a more significant change came in 1618 with the introduction of the *head right system,* which gave fifty acres to anyone paying their own way to Virginia plus another fifty acres for anyone else they brought. Finally, in 1623, all holdings were converted to private ownership.

Besides these problems, absentee direction added to the difficulties by limiting necessary local managerial direction. Institutional reforms in 1609 and 1612 increasingly gave those in Jamestown greater control over local matters. Shares in the company became based on labor input as well as capital contributions and planter memberships were created. A dep-uty governor was established in America to meet the prob-lems of leadership in a hostile environment and to generate more local autonomy. Authority and direction were steadily and increasingly decentralized. Such organizational changes, along with private ownership of property and a cash crop with a buoyant market, assured the permanence of the James-town colony.

Some of the difficulties of the Jamestown colony were avoided in the later settlements, for instance, in New England. Because the Massachusetts Bay Company actually carried its own charter to the New World, it thereby avoided absentee control and futile direction by English investors desiring immediate profits. Although much New England land was held in common, collective enterprise was not as forcefully imposed and private holdings increasingly replaced land held in common. Town corporations prolonged the use of common lands, but family farms emerged predominant after mid-century, even without the equivalent of an agricultural export staple.

Without exception investments in these early colonial ventures proved unrewarding. Indeed they were financial disasters. For instance, none of the investment by the Virginia Company, which totaled £200,000 by 1621, was ever repaid, neither principal or accumulated interest. Though losses on investments in the New England ventures were less, they too were financial failures, and London capitalists were heavy losers overall in their investments in the frontier.

Nevertheless the lessons of these first settlements served the British well in later ventures. One important change was to abandon the use of the joint stock company (except in settling Georgia, an unusual social experiment to be discussed below). The company arrangement had failed despite its facility in raising capital, partly because it was inadequate as a form of business management where decentralized organization and individual initiative were required. An essential factor for success in North America, along with permanent settlement and production for export, was the settler's stake in the land and individual participation in the direction of local affairs. As these needs were discovered, the use of monopoly privilege and company direction gave way to greater local control and management.

In addition, the award of Crown colonies or individually

owned proprietary colonies to supporters of the Crown during Cromwell's Protectorate increased for political reasons after the Restoration. All of the first settlements, including Virginia, Massachusetts, and New Hampshire, eventually became Crown colonies or proprietary colonies. Even New York, which was first settled by the Dutch West India Company and was then named New Amsterdam, became a proprietary colony after a small English fleet captured it in 1664 without firing a shot. In that year King Charles II granted it to his younger brother, the Duke of York. The proprietary arrangement had begun earlier, however, in 1632 when Maryland was granted to Sir George Calvert, later called Lord Baltimore; the Carolinas were given to Lord Ashley in 1663; New York, as mentioned, was transformed into a proprietary colony the following year, as was New Jersey; and Pennsylvania (including Delaware) was given as a proprietary colony in 1680 to William Penn.

Under this system a liberal land policy with decentralized local control was implemented. The institutional adjustments that introduced this new system came quickly and within two decades of first settlement the "company colony" based on trade monopoly had been abandoned.

Working the frontier

Although frontier hardships persisted, the early decades of starvation and disease eventually gave way to brighter periods of material comfort and by 1670, a mere half century after the landing of the Pilgrims, British North America could boast more than 100,000 residents. Mainland North America was now more than a mere collection of agricultural communities, fishing stations, and trading posts. Nevertheless, there were still ample stretches of unsettled territory, even at tidewater. Most of the people lived in either Massachusetts or Virginia. Philadelphia, which would be the largest city in North America a century later, was not yet established and almost no colonists lived in Pennsylvania.

Boston was the largest city with 4,000 inhabitants and New York was second with 3,000.

With no more than a couple of small towns, the colonial economy was overwhelmingly rural. It remained so throughout the entire colonial period. Even on the eve of the American Revolution, nearly 90 percent of the population made at least part of their living at farming. Essential subsistence farming activities, supplemented by lumbering, hunting, and fishing, were pervasive throughout the colonies. The abundance of land and natural resources relative to scarce labor and capital dictated the production of land- (and natural-resource) intensive products. Consequently, agriculture was the main economic activity in the colonies.

The most successful colonial regions were those whose products found buoyant markets in overseas areas. The major market, of course, was in Europe and as trade between the Old and New World expanded, specialized forms of production, based on regional comparative advantages, became clear. Generally there was much complementarity in exchange between the areas; with the Old World processing commodities and producing finished goods, colonies tended to specialize in primary products and raw materials. Although the two areas were interdependent, the limited diversification of the colonial economy and its overwhelming emphasis on primary production left it highly dependent on overseas markets for successful development.

Of course, not every colony was equally well endowed with fertile soil and warm climate, and there were substantial variations among regions in the particular patterns of agricultural development as well as great differences in the time pattern of development. Of all the colonial products, sugar enjoyed the most dynamic market in the mother country, but only the Caribbean colonies successfully cultivated sugar for export. The most important product from the mainland colonies was tobacco, the staple of the upper South—the Chesapeake colonies of Maryland and Virginia. In terms of value, tobacco remained the dominant export from the mainland colonies throughout the entire colonial period, and made up almost half the total value of commodity exports in 1750. Its share of total value of commodity exports was even higher in earlier decades but it began to ebb, falling to a low of 25 percent by the end of the period, as other products, such as rice, flour, fish, and indigo, increased in relative importance.

The expansive effect of tobacco production on the Chesapeake area can hardly be denied. In 1624, when the charter of the Virginia Company was revoked and Virginia became a Crown colony, the population of the upper South was about 2,500. By 1700 it had increased fortyfold, to approximately 100,000. The comparable growth of the major export staple, tobacco, was over 302 times, from a weight of 119,000 pounds in 1620 to nearly 36 million pounds in 1700. By the time of the Revolution tobacco exports had grown to over 100 million pounds annually, a sizable absolute increase, but this threefold growth clearly shows that the relative rate of expansion was slowing down.

The dynamic element in this commercial development, of course, was the European market. As the once-buoyant English market eventually became saturated, the market on the Continent continued to expand. Although the Navigation Acts listed tobacco (and other goods), and, in effect, required direct shipment of all tobacco to England, a liberal policy of reexport permitted an expansive market for tobacco on the continent.

Tobacco cultivation followed the various estuaries and navigable streams of the Chesapeake Bay area. Settlement remained tied to tidewater areas throughout the seventeenth century, but by the later eighteenth century much of the best tobacco land had been taken. To some extent this explains the slower expansion of tobacco in the eighteenth century, but the upper South continued to grow rapidly as the slackening increase in tobacco cultivation was offset by increased commercial production of grain along the Potomac, Rappahannock, York, and Roanoke rivers. By the late colonial period, the upper South was an important grain-producing region. In fact more acreage was devoted to Indian corn than to any other product; and both the tobacco plantations and small farms alike were self-sufficient in most foodstuffs, including vegetables and livestock as well as grain. For its own domestic consumption the region was well diversified so far as crop mix was concerned. In addition, the upper South sent beef and pork to some of the northern colonies, such as Pennsylvania and New York, and it also sent livestock and flour to the West Indies. Nevertheless, tobacco remained the dominant colonial export. Favored by suitable soil and climate and a safe natural harbor, the upper South reached a comparatively advanced state of specialized commercial agriculture.

The lower South, comprising the Carolinas and the youngest colony, Georgia (Florida was still Spanish), also enjoyed a substantial commercial success in agriculture. But development was noticeably uneven within this region. North Carolina experienced very limited growth, except for the northern tobacco areas bordering Virginia. The main problem was the lack of good harbors and navigable waterways, which made most of the better agricultural land in North Carolina inaccessible to cheap transport and therefore unsuitable for commercial development. Georgia was not colonized until the 1730s. As the last colony to be settled and acting as a buffer zone along the border of Spanish America, it also had limited commercial development until the late colonial period. Some corn and rice was commercially grown, near Savannah, but subsistence agriculture was the dominant characteristic of this new frontier. South Carolina, however, enjoyed substantial success by the early eighteenth century. Blessed with a safe harbor at Charleston and suitable conditions for rice production, South Carolina became the major rice-producing area of the colonies.

An expanding market first in the West Indies, then in Europe, north and south, boosted profits in rice production, but rice cultivation was extremely risky and technically troublesome. Initially, rice was cultivated in inland swamps that could be periodically flooded by nearby rivers. The uncertainty of stream flows made this procedure hazardous, however, and productive flat areas along the coast were eventually added by the use of dikes along the lower river areas. These dikes permitted proper flooding as fresh water was channeled into irrigation ditches by pressure from the ocean tides against the fresh water. This process demanded careful engineering to ensure against leakage of salt water. The constant care for the dikes and irrigation ditches made rice cultivation relatively *labor-intensive and capital-intensive* compared to tobacco and other forms of agriculture.

In 1743, Eliza Lucas, one of America's first female entrepreneurs, successfully introduced indigo to the lower South. Like rice, indigo production also required great skill, but it nicely complemented rice production because it could be grown on high ground where rice would not grow and its planting and harvesting times did not conflict with those of rice. Used to make dye for cloth, indigo was deemed so important in England that it was given a subsidy.

In addition to rice and indigo, the lower South exported naval stores such as pitch, turpentine, resin, hemp, tar, ship spars, and other fittings for ships. In fact the production of naval stores provided the major impetus to the early development of this region. But these were more in the nature of *extractive industries* than agriculture. By 1700, rice was the staple of the region and rice and indigo ranked third and fifth, overall, in terms of the value of total commodity exports from the mainland colonies in the late colonial period.

The region between the Potomac and the Hudson, including New York, New Jersey, Pennsylvania, and Delaware, comprised the middle colonies. The land of this area was fertile and easily tillable and gave a *comparative advantage* in grains and most foodstuffs. Known as the "bread colonies," this region produced substantial amounts of corn, wheat, rye, oats, and barley, and exported large quantities of flour. In the late colonial period these were second only to tobacco in terms of value of total commodity exports from the main-

land colonies. In addition to being the granary for its neighbors north and south, the middle colonies also produced
fruits and vegetables, especially potatoes, and they also exported quality livestock.

The major markets for middle-colonial goods were the
West Indies and Southern Europe, two areas with a rapidly
growing demand for wheat, bread, and flour, especially in
the eighteenth century. The burgeoning sugar plantations,
although capable of feeding themselves, had such an overwhelming comparative advantage in sugar production that it
was to their advantage to specialize in sugar and therefore to
import foodstuffs from the mainland. Consequently, the
growth of the sugar trade, based on expanding demand in
Europe, had important feedback effects on the mainland
colonies. These forces generated an expansive market for
foodstuffs, livestock, building materials, and other goods
that were supplied from the mainland. Consequently, although the middle colonies did not complement the mother
country by directly supplying substantial quantities of raw
materials to English manufacturers, they indirectly supported the empire's development by allowing the West Indies a greater degree of specialization through trade.

Least complementary in exchange with the mother country and least suitable for commercial agriculture was the
New England region. Despite extensive experiments with all
varieties of crops New England failed to produce any crop
with extensive overseas demand. Rocky soils and an inhos-
pitable climate permitted production only for subsistence
and local trade. Corn production was predominant by 1700,
though it was not significant commercially, and other grains,
apples, vegetables, and livestock production filled out the
pattern of farming. Rhode Island achieved limited distinc-
tion by producing horses for West Indian sugar mills, and
Connecticut also had a modest agricultural export base in
livestock, grain, salted meats, and dairy products.

Nevertheless, New England was a major trading area. New
Englanders, long since known for their "Yankee ingenuity,"

were able to develop a host of nonagricultural activities, such as extractive industries related to the sea and the forests, but also manufacturing and commercial activities. In fact the most valuable export from New England was shipping services, and in the late colonial period these services, in combination with the shipping services of the middle colonies, were more important than any of the commodity exports except for tobacco.

Colonial shippers played an important role in the empire, and the merchant marine of New England (and the middle colonies) was an important part of the empire's shipping from an early date. Moreover, the development of a viable commercial sector, in merchant activities as well as shipping, was an important sign of modernization and economic diversification. This development of a resident commercial sector contrasted sharply with the colonies south of Pennsylvania, and even more sharply with the limited commercial development in Spanish America.[3]

Besides being a carrier of others' produce, New England engaged extensively in the extraction of furs and other products from the forests and the sea. As we have emphasized, the market for furs in England was important in New England's early development. By 1650 or thereabouts, however, most of New England's furs had been depleted. Consequently, the fur trade was increasingly dominated by the French in the West and in Canada. Naval stores and lumber became important extractive industries, however, and the forest derivatives of pitch, tar, turpentine, masts, and yards, and the like were traded to England. Fishing and whaling were also important New England extractive industries, and the Catholic diet of Southern Europe provided an expanding market for high-quality fish, while the growing slave population in the West Indies supported a market for fish of lower quality. Consequently, New England fishing fleets regularly plied the fishing grounds of Newfoundland and the other maritime provinces and sold fish of all varieties on both sides of the Atlantic and throughout the Caribbean.

Because of the scarcity of labor and capital and the limited size of the market in the colonies, most manufactures were imported into the colonies. As a rule, efficient enterprises based on large-scale methods of production simply could not be supported there. An important exception, however, was the shipbuilding industry of New England, especially near Boston and Charlestown, although shipwrights also located in New York, Philadelphia, and even Baltimore. Shipbuilding was the only important industry that obtained significant competitive success against English manufactures. As early as 1660, export of large ships to England was the basis of a thriving New England industry, and by the end of the colonial period one-quarter to one-third of all British-owned vessels had been built in the colonies. In addition the market for ships in the colonies proved substantial, and even as early as 1700 the merchant fleet of New England, exclusive of fishing vessels, exceeded two thousand vessels.

The basis of the success of the New England shipbuilding industry was its proximity to raw materials. Despite the lower costs of labor and capital in England, the high costs of transport of bulky materials from the Baltic made ship construction comparatively more expensive in England. Higher wages in the colonies encouraged shipwrights to migrate to America, where they built vessels with low-cost materials at about two-thirds of British costs.[4] Consequently, shipbuilding was unusual because for most manufactures the relatively low costs of raw material in the colonies generally were not low enough to offset the much higher labor costs there. But in this case, the high costs of transport altered the comparative advantage of production in favor of the colonies. In addition, the Navigation Acts, discussed in Chapters 4 and 8, encouraged shipbuilding in the colonies.

Another case where the *natural tariff* of high transportation costs helped develop colonial manufacturing was in the sawmilling of lumber and in the production of crude and wrought iron. Crude iron, sometimes called pig or cast iron, was used mainly for pots, pans, and kettles, and wrought iron was used to make edged tools. Iron production in the colonies began in 1644 in Lynn, Massachusetts, but by the eighteenth century Pennsylvania was the most important center for iron production.

Pennsylvania was then the fastest growing colony and most of this iron production, like sawmilling, was for local use, not for export. Part of this success came because crude- and wrought-iron furnaces were small-scale operations requiring only a few skilled workers. Of course the British iron industry remained dominant, and supplied the colonies with most finished forms of iron and steel, but colonial iron production for the domestic market approached 15 percent of world output on the eve of the Revolution.

Lastly, all the colonies engaged in raw-material processing of one variety or another. Flour milling was extensive in the middle colonies, as was rum distilling in New England, mainly in Rhode Island. Hat making, glass fabrication, paper manufacture, and brickmaking on a small-scale basis and for local markets were other types of colonial manufactures. Textiles were also an important form of manufacturing employment, but not by way of factory production. Textile production in the households of the colonies was primarily of the homespun variety, passing through all stages from raw fiber to sewing the finished garment, and giving employment to women and children in the home. Dress goods and fashionable materials had to be purchased from England, but linsey-woolsey, a flax-wool combination, and jeans, a wool-cotton mixture, were the standard homemade apparel worn extensively in the North and West. Fustian, a cotton-flax blend, was a lighter fabric used in the South. Of course, various types of craftsmen and artisans also were to be found in the cities in the late colonial period.

Overall, however, nonagricultural activities employed only a small minority of the population. Limited market size and *labor and capital scarcity,* in conjunction with land and natural-resource abundance discouraged most types of manufactures and encouraged instead the production of land-intensive or natural-resource-intensive products. Consequently, agriculture preoccupied colonists, complemented by a variety of extractive industries, seafaring activities, and small-scale manufactures. Because of inadequate records and because the mainland colonists were famous for being jacks-of-all-trades, it is difficult accurately to proportion labor effort among these activities. But keeping in mind the wide variations among the regions as well as differences over time, probably as much as 80 percent of labor effort was devoted strictly to agricultural activities on the eve of independence. Most of this was for subsistence and self-sufficiency, but a significant degree of commercial agriculture was recorded in all the regions. Though a preindustrial economy, the colonies had reached a substantial degree of development in terms of their commercial sectors, especially in shipping and trade, and perhaps as much as 5 to 10 percent of the labor force was occupied in these activities. The remainder were engaged in the variety of extractive industries and manufactures described above.

Population expansion

Unquestionably, one of the most important features of British colonization and a critical factor in Britain's hold on the western frontier was the high rate of population growth in the colonies. A variety of forces powered a rate of population growth on the mainland that has seldom been matched, or even approached, in any other place or at any other time in history. Indeed, the rate of advance was so high–the population approximately doubled every twenty-five years–that Thomas Malthus called it "a rapidity of increase, probably without parallel in history."[5] According to Malthus and his followers, the American colonies were a prime example of a population that was growing virtually unchecked. They feared that such a rate of increase in Europe ultimately spelled pestilence, famine, and doom. These "dismal scientists" emphasized the obvious fact that the aggregate supply of land is fixed in amount.

Such European concerns were far from the minds of mainland colonists, however. On the frontier the main problem was not overpopulation, but rather underpopulation and labor scarcity, and this fact of American life persisted throughout the entire colonial period.

The broad aggregate trends of population growth are shown for each region in Figure 5. The rapid spurt of population growth in New England and the upper South in the earliest decades noticeably tapered off and assumed a slower but relatively steady path after 1640. The timing, rise, and levels of total population are remarkably similar for both regions. In contrast, the middle colonies and lower South, which developed later, displayed more rapid rates, thus allowing them to catch up somewhat with the front-runners. The steep trend in the lower South, the fastest-growing re-

Figure 5. Population growth of the thirteen colonies. *Source:* U.S. Bureau of the Census, *Historical Statistics of the United States, Colonial Times to 1957* (Washington, D.C.: Government Printing Office, 1960), p. 756.

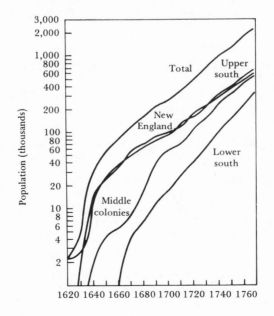

gion, is quite steady compared to the middle colonies, which experienced an unusually rapid surge between 1670 and 1690. However, despite these regional differences, in combination they produced a rise in the total population that was steady and showed no significant fluctuations after 1640.

Plentiful high quality land and suitable climate acted like a powerful magnet to attract Europeans and capture and ship Africans. Also the fruits of the land sustained an extremely high natural rate of increase of the resident population. It was this combination of high rates of immigration and natural increase that forged this unusual record and gave North America its greatest crop, its people.

The two forces of migration and natural increase changed roles over the period. Migration was the dominant source of population increase in the early decades of first settlement in each region. Therefore, regions of later settlement felt the strong forces of migration decades after they had waned in the more established regions. For each region, however, migration was the dominant source of population growth only in the first few decades. In New England, for instance, it was a minor source by as early as 1650.

From the evidence in Figure 6 on the percentage of the foreign-born in the black population, it appears that migra-

Figure 6. Foreign-born blacks as a percentage of the U.S. black population. *Source:* Robert W. Fogel and Stanley L. Engerman, *Time on the Cross* (Boston: Little, Brown, 1974), I, p. 23.

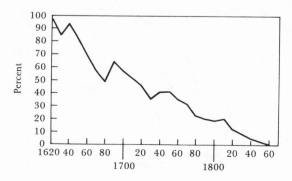

tion generally maintained a stronger role in the increase of blacks. By 1680 the number of foreign-born blacks on the mainland was less than those born in the New World. As shown in Figure 6, there was a temporary reversal in this ebbing role of migration around 1680, but by 1700 the natural rate of increase was clearly dominant in the growth of the black population.

The very limited role of migration in the white population is somewhat surprising in light of changes occurring in Europe. Nevertheless, once a modest degree of commercial success had been achieved in the colonies, then natural increases provided the main expansive force of population change. This shift, though delayed, was also true for the blacks, and as noted, this takeover came somewhat later in the middle colonies and lower South because of later settlement and for the lower South also because of the higher proportion of blacks in this region. For the white population as a whole, only about one-tenth were foreign-born on the eve of the Revolution. The comparable figure for blacks was nearly twice as high.

The high rate of population growth, of course, was partly determined by the high birth rate, which in North America was considerably above that in Europe. For instance, the average annual number of births per 1,000 population in the colonies in the eighteenth century ranged between 45 and 50, compared to perhaps 35 to 40 per 1,000 in England. A combination of demographic and economic forces explain these differences. Most migrants to the New World were young; thus the colonies had a higher percentage of the population of childbearing age. In addition colonists tended to marry earlier, with an average marrying age for women between twenty and twenty-three compared to an average in Europe nearer to twenty-five. Colonial men also tended to marry a few years earlier than European men, but as a rule men married a few years later than women. There were greater economic opportunities for an average young adult in the colonies and it was generally easier for young persons to strike out on their own, acquire land, and set up and maintain a household. Lower land costs in the colonies created this advantage and encouraged earlier marriages.

The earlier marriages and higher proportion of women of childbearing age in the colonies gave rise to an average of six or seven children per marriage compared to four or five per marriage in Europe. These higher birthrates per marriage resulted from the greater emphasis of rural economic activity stemming from a comparative advantage in agriculture. The overwhelmingly rural economic life of the colonies encouraged high birth rates because children in rural areas are typically less costly to raise than in urban places and their value in terms of their labor contribution tends to be greater.

The high birthrate alone, however, did not completely account for a rate of increase in the colonies twice that of Europe. Even more significant, once the early period of starvation had ended, was the exceptionally low mortality rate. The average number of deaths per 1,000 persons each year was between 20 and 25 in the colonies; in England the rate was probably between 25 and 35 per 1,000.

Part of this difference is explained by the lower average age of the American population and a lower proportion of people living in urban areas. Overall, Europe had proportionately more in the older age categories. But even more important was the relatively low mortality rate of colonial children. As a rule, colonial mothers were better fed and housed than those in Europe, and consequently their babies were healthier.

Despite superior medical technology in Europe the abundance of land and natural resources created a healthier environment for all persons, and longer lives in the colonies resulted. Food was more plentiful, and housing and fuel costs were much lower. This allowed most married adults to own their own houses in the colonies, and effectively combated the harsher winters in North America. In addition, epidemics rarely occurred in the colonies because of the healthier environment and lower population density in urban centers. Only the New England diphtheria epidemic in the late 1730s caused a jump in the usually low colonial mortality rates.

Once past childhood an average white male in the colonies could expect to reach his sixties, not too far below his mid-twentieth-century counterpart. Women, however, faced higher mortality rates because of the hazards of childbirth. Consequently their postchildhood life expectancy ranged in the forties.

Although the dominant role of immigration came only in the first few decades of settlement in each region, the period of greatest absolute migration flows came in the eighteenth century. In the seventeenth century the vast majority of white immigrants came from Britain, but there was a great falling off of migration from Britain after 1689. Finally, starting in 1768 a renewed surge created the greatest wave of British migration, and this lasted until the Revolution.

In the eighteenth century then, and especially after 1720, Scotch-Irish and German migrations provided the greatest numbers of white immigrants. Between 1718 and 1775 somewhere between 100,000 and 125,000 Scotch-Irish and nearly 100,000 Germans entered the mainland, mainly to the middle colonies.

In total, between 250,000 and 300,000 white immigrants entered the colonies from 1700 to 1775, contributing between 15 to 20 percent of the total increase in the white population. This contrasts with the much higher proportion in the black population, in which slave imports formed between one-third and two-fifths of the increase of the blacks in the eighteenth century.

The black migration is unique on several other counts as well. Its absolute magnitude was nearly as great as the total number of white immigrants from 1700 to 1775. Almost all these people went to the southern colonies, which contained 90 percent of the North American black population in the

1770s. Furthermore, the continued higher levels of black migration significantly altered the racial proportions of the general population. Between 1670 and 1770 the black share of the population rose from 4 to 20 percent.

As Figure 7 shows, important regional differences developed over the eighteenth century in the proportion of blacks in the population. By the end of the colonial period, South Carolina had the largest concentration of blacks, nearly 70 percent of the total population. In Virginia the proportion was 47 percent and 33 percent in Maryland. Because of the limited commercial development of North Carolina, due to inadequate harbors, the proportion of blacks was only 15 percent. In the northern regions the proportion was less than 5 percent.

The unusually high proportion of blacks in South Carolina resulted from the heavy use of slave labor in rice and indigo production. Slave labor was especially profitable in these lines of production because their planting and harvesting times did not coincide; thus slaves could be more fully occupied throughout the year. The favorable climate also allowed more workdays per year and longer hours. Consequently, South Carolina approached a social profile close to that indicated by the black concentrations in the French and

Figure 7. Blacks as a percentage of the total population in four regions. *Source:* Robert W. Fogel and Stanley L. Engerman, *Time on the Cross* (Boston: Little, Brown, 1974), I, p. 21.

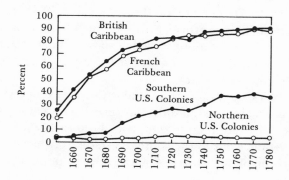

British Caribbean (Figure 7). This profile, unique to the mainland colonies, was a majority black population held in bondage and controlled by an elite white population of plantation owners.

The African migration matched the European migration from 1700 to 1775. During this period therefore, at least half of those coming to the American shores did so involuntarily. In addition at least half of the Europeans also arrived under various conditions of bondage. Indentured servants, or redemptioners, as they were sometimes called, accepted bondage voluntarily, however, and their economic, social, and legal status was far superior to that of the slaves. The promise of owning land, higher wages, and greater social mobility lured many Europeans from all walks of life, and according to Smith:

> Many . . . were convicts from the jails, transported instead of being hanged; a few were political and military prisoners taken in war or rebellion. There were rogues, vagabonds, whores, cheats, and rabble of all descriptions, raked from the gutter and kicked out of the country. There were unfortunate French, German, and Swiss Protestants fleeing from religious persecution, starving and unhappy Irish, rack-rented Scottish farmers, poverty-stricken German peasants and artisans, brash adventurers of all sorts. People of every age and kind were decoyed, deceived, seduced, inveigled, or forcibly kidnapped and carried as servants to the plantations. There were many ordinary individuals of decent substance, and a few who were entitled by the custom of the time to be called gentlemen.[6]

With inadequate savings and little possibility of borrowing, these persons willingly sold the rights to their labor services in order to pay for their passage to America. Typically they signed a contract with a shipowner or a recruiting agent, who in turn sold the contract to a planter or merchant once the ship arrived in the colonies. As a rule the period of bondage lasted four years, but it varied from two to seven years. Because most bonded servants were unskilled, this period of service was similar to a period of apprenticeship and in many ways was like an investment in education as well as an investment in migration. In return for their labor, bonded servants were given food, shelter, clothing, and "freedom dues," which sometimes included a mule and some land, at the end of their contract period.

Of course the life of an indentured servant could be harsh or pleasant depending on the whims of his or her task-master, but because of the scarcity of labor most servants worked under favorable conditions. Colonial courts upheld the rights of servants, and agents could not separate families, kidnapping was outlawed, and ship captains had to keep accounts of servants transported. Freedom was generally granted to the servant if a planter deviated from the contract agreement, and prior to 1774 the New York courts granted freedom to servants in every case alleging breach of contract. A runaway servant, however, would soon find that the forces of the law would swing the other way.

Redemptioners were a particular kind of indentured servant and generally had less favorable contracts. These individuals, mostly unskilled, non-English-speaking Germans, boarded ship without payment in the hope of making payment at the end of the voyage. When funds could not be raised, their weak bargaining position typically resulted in a contract of service of seven years with only minimal freedom dues.

The demand for indentured labor in the colonies was generally strong, especially in the middle and southern colonies, where more than half the white migrants came as bonded servants. Planters were happy to invest in these labor contracts because the labor of others generally made the difference between mere subsistence and material comfort for them.

As the changing structure of the population suggests, however, to many planters investments in slaves were more attractive than investments in indentured servants. This was not true in the northern colonies, but it was clearly evident in the southern regions, especially in the lower South. Probably because of capital constraints, most small planters continued to confine their purchases to servants, but wealthier planters increasingly concentrated in slaves.

This transition occurred throughout the entire South. In the mid-seventeenth century most purchased labor in the Cheasapeake region was indentured. Between 1670 and 1690, however, there was a shift in the relative position of slaves vis-à-vis servants, and by 1690 slaves outnumbered servants by two to one. That ratio continued to grow over the eighteenth century.

The buoyant demand for southern crops supported a strong demand for labor of all kinds. Efficient large-scale plantation operations, however, depended mainly, if not entirely, on slave labor. Moreover, indentured servants, especially the Germans, tended to prefer the middle colonies and did not migrate in sufficient numbers to match the demand for labor in the South. Increasingly slaves were substituted for bonded servants in the face of labor shortages and as rates of return on slave investments increased relative to rates of return on servant investments.

Meanwhile and earlier, laws were being passed that increasingly reduced blacks from human status to mere property. In 1669 the Virginia legislature decided that a master could not be punished even in the event of a slave's death due to maltreatment. Although such deaths undoubtedly occurred, the rationale behind the law was that it was deemed unthinkable that a master would voluntarily destroy his own property. By 1705 the slave code carefully defined the slave as nonhuman and as a form of property. These edicts stood in sharp contrast to the status granted by the courts to bonded white servants.

Efforts to contain slavery in the northern regions were aided by economic circumstances, but in southern colonies efforts to contain slavery usually were made in vain. A fascinating example of economic forces clashing with well-meaning social policy occurred in the establishment of South Carolina's sister colony, Georgia. In 1732 George II gave permission to a small group of public-spirited Englishmen led by James Oglethorpe to found such a colony, which was named Georgia after its royal patron. A keystone in the plan for the colony was a prohibition against slavery. The trustees hoped to ease urban pressures in England by offering economic opportunities to thousands of England's "urban wretches." The plan was to populate Georgia with thousands of freeholders employing indentured laborers on small, economically viable plantations. In this fashion, an all-white Georgia would not only ease urban population in England, but also act as a line of defense between the English colonies and Spanish Florida.

The antislavery policy was deemed essential to accomplish both the social engineering and a diplomatic coup. It was believed that if slavery were allowed, wages would be beaten down and cripple efforts to attract small farmers in large numbers. In addition slavery supposedly would encourage social unrest and possible rebellion. Events, however, disappointed the well-intentioned trustees because their praiseworthy moral and social objectives blatantly clashed with economic reality.

From the outset new arrivals in Georgia recognized the economic advantages of slave labor, and Georgian malcontents increasingly sent letters and petitions to the trustees advocating slavery. They argued that indentured servants could not or would not work as hard as slaves, were more vulnerable to the heat and cold of Georgia's climate, and could abscond too easily to another colony.

Prices alone actually favored the use of servants, and indentured contracts typically cost about one-fifth the purchase price of a slave (£6 per servant against £30 for a healthy young adult male slave). But slaves were worked until death whereas servants' contracts were usually only for four years. In addition slaves could be worked longer hours and more days per year, were able to produce valuable off-spring, and perhaps most importantly, required lower maintenance costs than servants.

Recent investigations indicate that the rates of return on investments in indentured servants in early Georgia were not above the prevailing interest rates on low-risk loans there; that is, *the opportunity cost of capital* and risk associated with investments in bonded servants therefore could not compensate for the differential. Investments in servants were not sufficiently profitable there. An economically viable colony based solely on indentured labor and large enough to serve as a military deterrent to the Spanish could not be created without outside subsidy. Consequently, a close look reveals that with or without slavery the aspirations of the trustees could not be realized. And yet, according to the trustees, a heavily black population, as in South Carolina, would not constitute an effective military buffer.

Eventually the futility of their plans was realized and by mid-century large waves of African laborers were pouring into Georgia. Slavery helped overcome labor scarcity. In the process Georgia quickly assumed the same general demographic characteristics of the other southern colonies, especially those of South Carolina.

Glossary of terms

Encomienda (commendation)
Encomienda is an arrangement whereby Spanish overseers extracted labor services from the native population. It was similar, but not identical, to slavery.

Property rights
Property rights are a societal institution that specifies who (a specific individual or group) has a legal claim to the ownership (and thereby a claim to the income produced) of any specific capital good or natural resource (property).

Mercantilism
Mercantilism was a set of governmental policies that existed from the sixteenth to the nineteenth centuries by which European gov-

ernments attempted to direct commerce so as to achieve power and wealth for various groups that held political power in the state (for more detailed explanation, see the discussion in Chapter 4).

Import substitution

The process by which one country produces more of a good itself, and therefore imports less of it. Usually this refers to manufactured goods, and it is part of the process of industrialization.

Headright system

A plan that granted fifty acres of land to anyone paying his or her ocean passage to Virginia, with a provision that another fifty acres could be obtained if the person paid the way for someone else.

Labor-intensive

Production processes characterized by the use of labor as the major input into production.

Capital-intensive

Production processes characterized by the use of capital goods as the major input into production.

Extractive industries

Those types of economic activities in which natural resources (other than agricultural land) comprise the major input into production.

Comparative advantage

The case in which one nation (usually because of its particular resource endowment) has a relative advantage in producing a good or service more cheaply than another nation. The advantage is relative (and not necessarily absolute) in the sense that the cost of production of the good or service in the first nation is less than the cost of production of that good or service in the second nation *relative* to the cost of production of other goods and services.

Natural tariff (referring to high transportation costs)

The barrier to trade that exists because high transportation costs make it uneconomic.

Labor scarcity

The situation that exists in one area when labor is less abundant, therefore relatively higher priced, than in another area.

Capital scarcity

The situation that exists in one area when capital is less abundant, therefore relatively higher priced, than in another area.

Opportunity cost of capital

Opportunity cost is the usual definition of economic cost. It refers to the alternative goods or services given up when a choice is made to produce a particular good or service. In other words, when resources are used to produce one certain good or service, society foregoes the opportunity of using those resources to produce other goods or services. Thus, cost is defined in terms of the alternatives sacrificed. The opportunity cost of capital refers to the sacrifice of the alternative of having more consumption goods that could have been produced from the resources that were used to produce the capital goods.

Selected readings

Bidwell, P. W., and J. I. Falconer, *History of Agriculture in the Northern United States, 1620–1860* (Washington, D.C.: Carnegie Institution, 1925).

Davis, Ralph, *The Rise of the Atlantic Economies* (Ithaca, N.Y.: Cornell University Press, 1973).

Galenson, David, "Immigration and the Colonial Labor System; An Analysis of the Length of Indenture," *Explorations in Economic History,* XIV, 4 (October 1977), pp. 360–77.

Gray, Lewis C., *History of Agriculture in the Southern United States to 1860* (Washington, D.C.: Carnegie Institution, 1933), Volume I.

Gray, Ralph, and Betty Wood, "The Transition from Indentured to Involuntary Servitude in Colonial Georgia," *Explorations in Economic History,* XIII, 4 (October 1976), pp. 353–70.

Shepherd, James F., and Gary M. Walton, *Shipping, Maritime Trade, and the Economic Development of Colonial North America* (Cambridge: Cambridge University Press, 1972), Chapters 3, 8.

4

The ascent of commerce

The commerce of the American colonies took place within an institutional setting called mercantilism. In this chapter, after defining mercantilism more elaborately than we did earlier in Chapter 3, we examine British economic development in the broader setting of the Atlantic economy during the seventeenth and eighteenth centuries. Then we look at colonial commerce, with special emphasis upon overseas trade and shipping during the latter part of the American colonial period.

Mercantilism and the American colonies

Britain's colonial policies were part of a larger body of economic ideas and imperial laws that have come to be called "mercantilism" by historians. This concept was once regarded simply as the identification of wealth with money. The goal of mercantilism was said to be the promotion of exports and discouraging of imports, to produce a *favorable balance of trade*. The result, an inflow of specie and bullion into a country, would increase the nation's money supply, or "wealth." While it is true that "much contemporary thinking about economic matters was influenced by a concern for the balance of trade . . . , "[1] the modern study of mercantilism incorporates many more complex concerns than a mere balance sheet of trade. In fact, current scholars do not completely agree about even the basic premises underlying the emergence of the policies.

Nineteenth-century German scholars, and more recently the great Swedish economic historian, Eli Heckscher, have credited the origins of mercantilist policy to groups wanting to obtain or retain political power.[2] As in the rise of nation-states in early modern Europe, they assert, national economic interest was subordinated to political motivation. Jacob Viner has criticized this view, preferring to regard mercantilism as a system in which economic, and especially commercial, considerations were at least as important as political interests; he notes that wealth and power mutually support one another.[3] The economic interests of various groups might not fully coincide, but the national economic interest, as seen by those holding political power, did play a major role in the formulation of mercantilist policies.

Others, such as Adam Smith, with some justification have described mercantilism as a system where commercial interests pursued market position and monopoly power.[4] On another score, the fiscal needs of the state clearly played a role: When English mercantile and shipping earnings increased as a result of active domestic trade, the state stood to benefit from greater tax levies on commerce. Yet another view has been expressed by John Maynard Keynes, who saw the mercantilists as forerunners of his own *macroeconomic analysis*. Asserting that inadequate aggregate demand causes the underemployment of resources, Keynes suggested that in emphasizing policies that spurred demand, the mercantilists were stimulating trade, employment, and mercantile profits instead of single-mindedly pursuing the goal of economic efficiency. Then there is the view of mercantilism as a system whereby one country attempts to exploit another by means of trade.

Whatever the final decision may be on the origins of mercantilism, it is beyond the scope of these few brief comments to harmonize all the issues involved. Clearly, there is some truth in many of these views and interpretations, but most historians would agree with Viner that economic interests were basic in mercantilism's formulation.

Our concern here, of course, is simply that British mercantilist ideology and policies provided the framework within which colonial trade took place. It is enough to say at this
point that these policies evolved as a general framework of
economic organization for Britain in a world of competitive
and often hostile Western European nation-states. In such a
world it made good sense to seek some degree of self-sufficiency in those pursuits important to national security and
economic welfare. For example, a strong merchant marine
could contribute to a nation's naval strength in time of war,
supplying ships and experienced seamen to safeguard its
ocean borders.

It also made sense that national economic interests might
best be served by promoting the market position of one's
own producers, merchants, and shippers. This was true because in much of that period any changes in relative productivity between nations occurred very slowly; therefore, production was normally viewed as a "fixed pie" to be split
among those in a position to affect its slicing. A larger share
of the pie would go to the nation that could increase exports: not only would its own domestic production flourish,
but it could also enjoy more imported goods with the earnings from exports and from mercantile and shipping services sold to foreigners.

What British policies most notably affect the economic development of the American colonies? Perhaps most critical
was that part of mercantilist legislation called the Navigation
Acts. During the English Civil War (1642–9) the colonies
had developed the "bad" habit of shipping directly to Continental markets, depriving English merchants of this trade
and its profits. To counter such activities, the Navigation
Acts, beginning with the act of 1651, were passed by Parliament under the Protectorate. The first act, focusing on imports, stated that merchandise must be brought to Britain
directly from the country of production (or the port where
usually first shipped), either in English ships or in ships of
the country of origin (or of usual first shipment). Most im-

portant to the colonies, no goods could be imported into England from Asia, Africa, or America in foreign ships.

Far more crucial to the colonies, however, was a later series of acts. These were to establish the framework within which the overseas trade of the colonies could and would be carried out (with minor additions and modifications) for the remainder of the American colonial period. Acts passed by Parliament from 1660 through 1662 included the following three stipulations:

1. All trade of the colonies was to be carried in vessels that were English-built and owned, commanded by an English captain, and manned by a crew three-quarters of whom were English sailors. "English" was defined as "only his Majesty's subjects of England, Ireland, and the Plantations." Of great importance to colonists was the fact that colonists and colonial ships were both considered "English" under Navigation Acts.

2. All foreign merchants were excluded from dealing directly in the commerce of the English colonies. They could engage in colonial trade only through England and merchants resident there.

3. Certain commodities produced in the colonies could be exported only to England (or Ireland, Wales, Berwick-on-Tweed, or other English colonies – essentially any destination within the empire). These "enumerated" goods included such items as sugar, tobacco, cotton, indigo, ginger, and various dyewoods (such as fustic, logwood, and braziletto). The list was amended and lengthened over the remainder of the colonial period.

Another act passed in 1663 reiterated the provision of the act of 1651: goods produced elsewhere in Europe and destined for the colonies must first be sent to England (or Wales or Berwick) before being shipped to the American colonies. A few exceptions permitted direct importation of indentured servants, horses, provisions from Scotland or Ireland, wine from Madeira and the Azores, and salt for the northern fisheries. These, too, were modified over the rest of the colonial period. In 1707 the union of Scotland and England gave Scottish citizens the same privileges as English ones. Henceforth, after 1707 "English" was interpreted as "British" in the above laws.

Later mercantilist legislation supplemented the basic Navigation Acts. The export of wool from the colonies and the colonial production of hats were restricted. In the 1750s, the construction of new iron-slitting mills was prohibited. The Molasses Act of 1733 levied a prohibitive duty on molasses imported into the colonies from the foreign West Indies (fortunately for the American colonies this act was never strictly enforced and apparently did little to damage colonial trade).

As every student of the American Revolution knows, various revenue acts passed after 1763 did indeed affect that trade and raised the ire of colonists. Ostensibly intended to cover the increasing costs of administering and defending the colonies, the acts were enforced energetically and effectively. The Sugar Act, in 1764, set realistic duties on sugar and molasses imported from the foreign West Indies. The Stamp Act, in 1765, required revenue stamps to be affixed to contracts, deeds, wills, and newspapers. The Townshend Act, in 1767, reorganized the customs system and promulgated stricter enforcement of customs rules, while also levying a duty on glass, lead, tea, and paper imported into the colonies. (These acts, designed to raise revenue for the Crown, will be discussed further in Chapter 8.) Quite different were the acts passed at various times, whose purpose was to promote colonial production of certain commodities by granting bounties or subsidies. Naval stores and indigo may have benefited from such concessions, but not all promotions were equally successful. A bounty offered on hemp, for example, did little to establish this as a viable crop in the colonies.

Such was the legal framework that encompassed colonial

trade. There may always be a slip " 'twixt the cup and the lip" in any sort of regulation of economic activity. Certainly, this was true of mercantilism. Keeping in mind these restrictions, let us turn to an examination of British economic development and the trade of the American colonies.

British economic development and colonial trade

At the time America was discovered, England was an underdeveloped country in comparison with the major European countries and areas. Its population was considerably smaller than that of France or Italy. Agriculture and other primary types of production were more important in its economy than manufacturing, in contrast to more advanced areas in Italy, the Low Countries, and southern Germany. English foreign trade, like that of present-day "underdeveloped" countries, was characterized at the end of the medieval period by exports of raw materials, most importantly, raw wool. Foreign merchants controlled, and foreign-owned ships carried, most of these goods. Though some manufactured goods like woolen cloth were exported, no one living then would have suspected that not quite three centuries later, English industrialization would burst from its shell so explosively that historians would later term it the Industrial Revolution. Needless to say, other areas that together with England were later to form Great Britain – Scotland and Wales – were then even less developed than England.

The English economy was soon to undergo profound changes. After 1500, production and export of woolen textiles accelerated until, by 1600, this was England's chief export. Iron and coal production, so important a base to later industrialization, increased rapidly after the mid-sixteenth century. New technology, some imported from the more industrially advanced Continent, but much of it developed domestically, expanded the production and use of iron and coal in more processes and products. Also, England became the fortunate refuge of many foreign religious dissidents who brought with them knowledge and skills of industrial processes.

Related developments affected the service sector. By the middle of the sixteenth century, English merchants had replaced most foreign shippers in English commerce. Similar trends occurred in finance. On the oceans, England won her rank as a great naval power by defeating the Spanish Armada in 1588, but it should be remembered that the English merchant marine was growing equally vigorously in that same sixteenth century in the lee of naval strength. London emerged as a powerful center of commerce, finance, and insurance, while smaller English towns also prospered from the growing commercialization. Although the changes were not of the magnitude that took place after 1750, the foundations for industrialization were being laid in this early modern period by the transformation of the English economy. Some economic historians, like John U. Nef, have even termed this earlier period a "first industrial revolution."

Such profound alterations were accompanied by tremendous growth in the volume of trade and by a shift in its composition to reflect the growing commercialization, industrialization, and diversification of the English economy. This brings us to the central topic of this chapter: the development of the Atlantic trade and economy in which the American colonies held such a key position.

British overseas trade

The lack of statistical data on English foreign trade for the seventeenth century makes it difficult to say by how much English exports grew over the period 1600 to 1775, but some estimates may be made for the earlier years. Approximations for 1601 and 1640 have been derived by Minchinton, based upon evidence presented by Fisher for 1601 and 1640, and by Davis for later periods.[5] Table 3 shows the following expansion in England's export trade over this period:

Table 3

1601	£1 million
1640	1.6–1.8 million
1699–1701	6.4 million
1722–4	7.8 million
1752–4	11.9 million
1772–4	15.7 million

The earlier figures are to be taken very tentatively, and Davis believes that exports in 1640 may have been as high as £2.5 to £3 million.[6] Nevertheless the figures indicate that, although growth in English foreign trade over this period was by no means uniform, the longer-term trends were vigorously upward.

One should note that these data for 1699–1774 apply only to England and Wales (and it was not until after 1774 that Wales with its coal, iron, and copper made any significant contribution to English overseas trade). Scotland's foreign trade statistics were kept separately, even after the Act of Union in 1707. Though Scottish trade was not large in the seventeenth century, it grew during the eighteenth to levels of consequence – the Glasgow tobacco trade, as we shall see, was very important, especially to the American colonies. Hence, if the above figures had referred to all of Great Britain rather than to England alone, the growth shown would be even greater.

As late as 1640, woolen cloth had comprised 80 to 90 percent of English exports. But from that date into the eighteenth century to 1775, the character and composition of English trade underwent a complete transformation. Table 4 gives some idea of these alterations.[7]

Although exports of woolen cloth increased absolutely during this period, the obvious decline in its relative importance shows how rapidly exports were expanding in other categories.

The earliest notable change, after 1640, was a surge in reexports–that is, goods first imported, then exported in much the same form to a different overseas destination. Such activities, although no direct stimulus to domestic production, benefit mercantile and ancillary services of distribution, such as shipping and marine insurance. As a proportion of total exports, reexports rose from 3 or 4 percent in 1640 to 31 percent around 1700 and to 37 percent in the 1770s.

The growth of the reexport trade in the latter part of the seventeenth century largely was due to the exchange of three commodities produced within the British empire– sugar, tobacco, and Indian calicoes–for which there was a huge potential demand in European markets if only cheaper sources could be developed. Sugar had been known to Europeans since ancient times, but until the colonization of the Americas it was extremely scarce and expensive, so that honey had been used as the common sweetener. During the fifteenth century, sugar production was developed in Madeira, the Canary Islands, São Tomé, and other Portuguese islands in the Atlantic. The Spanish were the first to establish sugar production in the New World in the early sixteenth century on the Caribbean island of Española (present-day Hispaniola), and more than a century passed before the English began to plant cane commercially on the island of

Table 4

	ca. 1700	ca. 1773
Woolen cloth	47.5%	26.7%
Other manufactured goods	8.4	27.4
Foodstuffs	7.6	3.7
Raw materials	5.6	5.1
Total exports of domestic production	69.1	62.9
Reexports	30.9	37.1
Total exports	100.0	100.0

Barbados. Established by English entrepreneurship and capital, and cultivated by slaves brought from Africa, sugar had become the New World's most valuable export to England by the beginning of the eighteenth century. Settlement of the other West Indian islands of St. Christopher (now St. Kitts), Nevis, Montserrat, Antigua, and Jamaica followed, and soon the British West Indies was one of the brightest jewels of the empire because of its sugar trade. Shipments grew from 15 million pounds per year in the 1660s to 37 million pounds at the turn of the century. After that time, competition from the French and others caused British reexports of sugar to the Continent to slow down by the 1730s. Demand in the British Isles (including Ireland) continued strong, however, presenting the sugar producers of the British West Indies with a continually growing market.

The previous chapter has described tobacco production in Virginia, Maryland, and northern North Carolina. We recall that it was first grown, in 1612, as an experiment by John Rolfe in Jamestown, in the hope of finding some product that could be exported by the infant colony in return for English imports to brighten the lives of the new inhabitants and perhaps even generate some profits for shareholders in the Virginia Company. Rolfe had probably not reckoned on Europe's quick addiction to "the weed," but the colonies were quick to recognize its potential as an export. Tobacco production spread like wildfire throughout the tidewater areas of Virginia, and then Maryland, as settlement proceeded over the seventeenth century. Tobacco imports into London rose from about 50,000 pounds in 1618 to more than 7 million pounds by the early 1660s (an increase of 140-fold); it then more than quadrupled between the 1660s and the end of the century to over 30 million pounds. Unlike sugar, tobacco proved to be a self-sustaining, marketable product on the Continent; thus it became not only a highly profitable export for the colonies and a principal commodity for English domestic consumption but also, and more importantly, a cherished part of the reexport trade.

Though interrupted at times by the many wars of the eighteenth century, the tobacco trade was so strongly supported by demand that it continued to expand through the whole period. After the Act of Union in 1707, Scottish tobacco firms gradually came to control an increasingly larger proportion of the exports of the tobacco colonies. By the early 1770s, Great Britain was importing about 100 million pounds of tobacco, and more than 85 percent of this was being reexported to Continental markets in the late colonial period.

The third major commodity in the rapidly expanding English reexport trade of the second half of the seventeenth century was calico from India. As the English were to learn later during their own Industrial Revolution, consumers around the world had a seemingly insatiable demand for a cheap, light, and washable cotton cloth. Calicoes produced by low-paid Indian handloom weavers first tapped this market, then became an important fraction of England's reexport trade during the later seventeenth century. After 1700, the trade was restricted by other European governments seeking to protect their own domestic textiles.

Together these three commodities at the turn of the eighteenth century produced two-thirds of the value of English reexports, while two-thirds of their total quantities went to European markets. The burgeoning reexport trade of the eighteenth century also became more diversified, to include important new commodities like coffee, tea, silks, German linens, rice, and dyestuffs. Tobacco, however, held its place as the single most important good in Britain's reexport trade right up to the American Revolution, comprising over 15 percent of all English reexports in the early 1770s. If Scotland's reexports are added to England's (40 million pounds per year from 1771 to 1775 compared with 46 million pounds for England for the same period), the British reexports of tobacco reach an even more impressive total.

Two other mercantile activities, the slave trade and the Newfoundland fishery, do not show up in the foregoing trade statistics for England. Like reexports, the trade in

Newfoundland codfish involved the product of a colonial overseas area; however, in this case the product (codfish) was exported directly to foreign markets, which in the eighteenth century were principally in Southern Europe and the West Indies. Even so, English merchants enjoyed a joint participation with colonial merchants in this trade and it brought them shipping earnings and mercantile profits. This was even more true of the slave trade, where the transport of Africans to the West Indies and to southern Continental colonies for sale to plantation owners was largely in English hands.

A third major development in the English export trade is apparent in the foregoing table. Largely because of demand from the American colonies, English manufactured goods other than woolen textiles were on the rise in the export trade after 1660. By 1700 they still produced little more than 8 percent of the total English trade, but by the 1770s their share had risen to more than 27 percent. This category included fabricated metal products such as tools and cooking vessels; also glass and earthenware, paper, hats, linen, and a whole array of colonial needs. Exports from London, which amounted to an annual £222,000 in the 1660s, had risen to £420,000 by around 1700. Although this period precedes the classical "Industrial Revolution," it is clear that such exports reflected a gradual industrialization and diversification in the English economy.

The demand for these manufactured English goods increasingly stemmed primarily from the American colonies and secondarily from Ireland and India. A relative decrease in the importance of European markets is evident in the following English export trade figures:

	ca. 1700	*ca. 1773*
Northern Europe	52.3%	31.8%
Southern Europe	26.6	17.0
Other British Isles	5.7	13.3
America	13.3	32.9
East India	2.1	5.0

By the early 1770s, about a third of English exports were traveling to the American colonies and more than half to destinations within the empire. Brinley Thomas has called this shift in English trade during the eighteenth century the "westernization effect" because of the important expansion of exports to Ireland as well as to the American colonies.[8] Through the century and until the Revolution, exports to European markets were increasing in absolute terms, but colonial markets absorbed 72 percent of the increase in English exports from 1700 to the early 1770s and the American colonies alone accounted for nearly half of this increase. By the time of the Revolution, America was a highly valuable customer for Britain.

On the other side of the balance, America and other colonial areas were gaining importance as suppliers to Britain. The changing relative importance of various overseas areas during the eighteenth century is illustrated by the following figures on English imports:

Imports from:	ca. 1700	ca. 1773
Northern Europe	34.2%	22.4%
Southern Europe	26.6	14.4
Other British Isles	7.4	10.7
America	18.9	37.4
East India	12.9	15.1

This increasing utilization of colonial products was, of course, a goal both of the Navigation Acts and of overall British mercantilist policy. It was also an outgrowth of the spreading industrialization of the British economy. More and more, Britain was producing manufactured goods from imported raw materials and in this transition the American colonies played a key role, shipping to the mother country a wide array of primary goods from their abundance of natural resources. Foodstuffs, also, were assuming more importance in English imports during the eighteenth century, as evidenced in the following figures:

Imports of:	ca. 1700	ca. 1773
Manufactured goods	31.7%	16.9%
Foodstuffs	33.6	50.9
Raw materials	34.7	32.9

Such trends were clearly those of an economy gaining sophistication and manufacturing skills. In the exchange of goods, Great Britain and the colonies provided reciprocal markets: American exports, tobacco above all, found ready acceptance both in Britain and as a reexport to the Continent, whereas the colonies eagerly welcomed manufactured goods from British mills and factories and such reexports as silks, tea, German linens, and a variety of other foreign-produced merchandise. In the process, fleets of ships moved across the ocean, and the trade winds blew briskly for the eighteenth-century economy on both sides of the Atlantic. These trends in British overseas trade and in the development of the British economy lead to a conclusion that the Navigation Acts (aided to some extent by the wars with the Dutch) were effective in channeling colonial trade away from foreign merchants and shippers and to English ones. As described in the preceding section, the acts formulated between 1651 and 1664 were not importantly modified before 1786. Initially they served to assure to English merchants and shipowners, and to some degree to colonists, a monopoly over colonial trade they would not otherwise have held during the second half of the seventeenth century.

Had the colonies remained free to trade directly with Continental countries, a trade network of direct routes would undoubtedly have developed. Because Amsterdam was the chief European entrepôt for trade as well as the principal European financial center around 1660, and because the Dutch were more competitive in providing ocean shipping services over most routes, it seems probable that they would have claimed the lion's share of colonial trade, perhaps even to the extent of handling those exports going to England itself. As it was, most of the British mercantile and shipping services, as well as the trade goods themselves, became the best bargain the colonists could obtain. Certainly the custom of trading with British firms became well established during the eighteenth century and continued even after the Revolution, as we shall see in Chapter 9.

Clearly, then, the Navigation Acts were directly responsible for a part of England's dominant trading position with the Continental seaboard colonies, which lasted well into the nineteenth century. But this advantage was enormously strengthened by another circumstance dating back to the mid-seventeenth century. At that time, just emerging from a series of civil wars, England discovered that while she had been preoccupied on the home front, the Dutch had seized control of the profitable reexport trade. Under mercantilist guidelines, England promptly set about to reclaim the trade by force, and in 1664 the resulting hostilities cost the Dutch the vital American foothold of "New Amsterdam" – New York.

Some historians of the American colonial period claim that the Navigation Acts loaded a costly economic burden on the colonists. (This is a different question, which will be addressed in Chapter 8.) Certainly they did serve to distort trade to some extent, primarily in respect to tobacco produced in America that had to be shipped first to Britain before reaching its ultimate market on the Continent. We can estimate the amount of this distortion by examining the pattern of trade following the American Revolution, when the new United States could finally trade freely and directly with Continental Europe, and we shall look into this situation in Chapter 9.

For the time, however, Britain held indisputable control of American trade and shipping and had drastically cut into Dutch shipping by invading, again, the reexport trade. Partly as a result, London soon replaced Amsterdam as Europe's foremost financial center and entrepôt. Changes were taking place, too, in the relative importance of different commodities and different overseas routes. Exports of a wide variety of manufactured goods stimulated trade in the eighteenth century; and on an ever-increasing scale British trade within the empire, and especially with the American colonies, played a crucial part in British economic development.

Colonial markets: trade and participation in the Atlantic economy from the American point of view

Today's economists can rejoice over one byproduct of mercantilist policy. Because Britain was so concerned in the eighteenth century over the colonies' commercial activities, we have a chance to inspect the ledgers of the American Inspector General[9] – a comprehensive listing of all the commodities and quantities entering into the legal trade of the British-American colonies in the years 1768 through 1772. Together with other evidence, these data let us examine the magnitudes, patterns, and composition of overseas trade and other economic relationships of the late colonial period.

As we turn now to a fairly detailed examination of this combined evidence, it is well to keep in mind the patterns of regional specialization described in Chapter 3; these, jointly with the evidence, will help us better understand the various kinds of economic activities taking place in each colonial region. The ledger entries must be treated with some caution, recalling that they pertain principally to overseas trade (not to that taking place within or among the colonies, nor to the large amount of subsistence production) and that they may not be wholly accurate. With that proviso, it can be said that they surely capture the broad patterns of trade in the late colonial period.

Estimates of colonial exports from the thirteen colonies based upon the American customs records provide the following annual average magnitudes for the period 1768–72:

Great Britain	£1,528,000
Ireland	87,000
Southern Europe	406,000
West Indies	759,000
Africa	21,000
Total	£2,801,000

Exports to Britain were thus valued at more than to all the other overseas areas combined, accounting for 55 percent of the value of all exports, as against 27 percent to the West Indies and 14 percent to Southern Europe. Ireland and Africa were relatively unimportant in the direct commodity export trades. Historians have generally overemphasized the importance of the African trade: as shown in this table, exports to Africa averaged less than 1 percent of the total value of colonial exports in this five-year period. The immorality and inhumanity of the slave trade, and of those relatively few northern colonists who engaged in it, were clearly abhorrent, and it is evident that the value of black slaves brought into the colonies from Africa was significant. Nevertheless, since commodity exports to Africa were negligible, it appears that the slave trade was largely in the hands of the British – not of the colonists.

Regional implications for the colonies' export trade may be found in the figures for 1768–72. The value of each colonial region's export trade with each overseas area is given as a percentage of the value of that region's total export trade (Table 5).

Basically, these percentages show the relative importance of each overseas area as a trading partner with each colonial region. The most striking fact evidenced is that by far the greatest part of exports from the southern colonies went to

Table 5

Area	Great Britain and Ireland	Southern Europe	West Indies	Africa
New England	18%	14%	64%	4%
Middle colonies	23	33	44	0
Upper South	83	9	8	0
Lower South	72	9	19	0
Thirteen colonies	58	14	27	1

Great Britain with some share to Ireland, whereas New England and the middle colonies found markets for their products principally in other areas overseas – namely, the West Indian islands and some parts of the Caribbean mainland, and in the countries of Southern Europe. As seen in Chapter 3, the southern colonies were highly successful in producing commodities for export directly to Great Britain to pay for the many goods they wished to import. The northern colonies, on the other hand, chose to specialize in the production of foodstuffs and raw materials for the West Indies and Southern Europe. The West Indian islands, as we have seen in the previous section, had by this time discovered that the production of sugar and other tropical and semitropical crops for export offered the most efficient use of their resources; thus they imported the bulk of their food requirements from the British North American colonies and this West Indian trade was of greatest importance to the New England area. Southern Europe, another area deficient in foodstuffs and the third-ranking colonial trading area, drew its supplies largely from the middle colonies.

The composition of the export trade lends additional insights into these patterns of trade. The annual average values of the five most valuable commodities exported during 1768–72 were

Tobacco	£766,000
Bread and flour	410,000
Rice	312,000
Fish	154,000
Indigo	113,000

These five comprised nearly 63 percent of the total value of colonial exports at this time. The southern staples – tobacco, rice, and indigo – were paramount in the southern colonies' large direct trade with Great Britain. Foodstuffs, and such other raw materials as lumber and wood products, formed the basis of the West Indian and Southern European trades. Exports of bread and flour (largely the latter) were second only to tobacco in value and show why the middle colonies were sometimes called the "bread" colonies. Exports of fish came primarily from New England. Other commodity exports to Great Britain worthy of mention were deerskins from the back country (especially from South Carolina); naval stores (tar, pitch, and turpentine) from the sandy pine forests of North Carolina; whale oil from New England; bar and pig iron, principally from Pennsylvania and Virginia; and potash. Flaxseed from the middle colonies was the single most important export to Ireland. Other foodstuffs, such as corn, wheat, and salted meat (both beef and pork) were important exports to the West Indies and Southern Europe, together with livestock, wood products, and spermaceti candles. Cotton was not to become an important export until later, and what small amounts were included in overseas trade had usually been already imported from the West Indies.

Descriptions of the colonial economy generally have emphasized the importance of commodity production while ignoring (or, at best, downgrading) the transportation and mercantile activities arising from the distribution of these commodities. By the late colonial period, substantial income was being generated by what are termed the "invisible earnings" of trade: those from the provision of shipping and distributional services. From 1768 to 1772, shipping earnings alone were £600,000 – a greater sum than was being brought in by any single trade commodity except tobacco.

Table 6

Area	Great Britain and Ireland	Southern Europe	West Indies	Africa
New England	66%	2%	32%	0%
Middle colonies	76	3	21	0
Upper South	89	1	10	0
Lower South	86	1	13	0
Thirteen colonies	79	2	20	0

And when this amount is added to the other invisible earnings, such as merchants' profits, insurance, and interest (altogether, probably well over £200,000 annually during the period), the total surpassed even the tobacco trade. As a matter of fact, the sale of such services to overseas buyers was a major source of foreign exchange to the colonies, helping to balance their deficits in commodity trade with Great Britain (as we shall see in Chapter 5) and comprising a major share of colonial market activity. It is difficult to overemphasize their importance, especially for the New England colonies, which earned over 54 percent of all colonial shipping returns.

The other side of the picture of colonial overseas trade is, of course, imports. Here the story is somewhat different than for the export trades. All colonial regions imported primarily from Great Britain; imports from the West Indies, especially into New England and the middle colonies, were of secondary importance. Imports from Southern Europe were very small, as can be seen from the percentages in Table 6 showing the share of each region's commodity imports from each overseas area for 1768–72.

The most valuable goods of British and Irish manufacture imported into the colonies were linens and woolens of various sorts, and the various metals, primarily brass, copper, and iron, which were wrought or cast into finished wares, such as nails, pots and pans, and tools. A wide range of lesser imports included wearing apparel, for example, hats and haberdashery; other sorts of household goods, such as glassware, earthenware, and china and pewter utensils; gunpowder and shot; paper; silk; leather and leather goods; and drugs. This diversity is illustrated in an invoice dated August 5, 1770, sent to the Philadelphia firm of Reynell and Coates from the English manufacturing firm of Welch, Wilkinson & Startin of Birmingham, England. The original order, sent through a Bristol merchant named William Seede, had been to ship on board the first vessel bound for Philadelphia the following motley array of goods:

buttons, vests, buckles, boxes, brass buckles, oval buckles, chapes, shovels & tongs, 5 small br'ad screw gimblett, saws – whet & sett, sash pullies, brass ink potts, hand saw files, inch shoe rasps, smiths vices, stone wyre, dead stock locks, padlocks, sheep shears, boucles, candlesticks, dotted awl blades, shoe tacks, steel buckles, pen knives, pistol cap'd pocket knives, sham buck table knives, flatt rough files, chest locks, cloth colour'd and blew thread, money scales, common snuffers, steel knees, shapper bellows, hunters whips, window cords, . . . [10]

And the list went on and on. The commodities in demand for reexport from Great Britain to the colonies included tea, hemp, German and Russian linens, and various spices and drugs, together with a host of less valuable items. Perhaps the best short description of the import trade from Britain and Ireland has been given by a Philadelphia merchant, who wrote that imports from Britain included

all kinds of British manufactories in great abundance and India goods, etc. In the last of the winter or early spring [we] choose to import our linens and other things fit for summer, the latter end of which we should have our woolen goods of all kinds ready for the fall sale to use in winter. The spring is the best time for iron mongery, cutleryware, furniture for furnishing houses, and all other brass and iron work. Our imports of those articles are very large, the people being much employed in agriculture, husbandry, clearing and improving lands, but slow progress is made in the manufactories here.[11]

This import trade from Great Britain and Ireland averaged £3,083,000 per year for the period 1768–72, dwarfing imports from all other overseas areas. During this period British and Irish imports were over four times the value of commodity imports from all other areas combined: 90 percent of these goods came from England, about 9.5 percent from Scotland, and less than 0.5 percent directly from Ireland. Clearly England held the dominant position in supplying imports to the colonies, and most of these (about 80 percent of English exports to the colonies) were goods of English manufacture, with textiles easily heading the list. Judging from the official values in the English customs records, woolens comprised about 40 percent of the value of all goods of British manufacture, and linens about 25 percent (including Irish linens reexported from England). Hardware and metal goods of all shapes and descriptions comprised another 15 percent. German linens, for which import duties in England were rebated upon reexport to the colonies, were a popular item, amounting to about 16 percent of the total value of English reexports to the colonies. Tea comprised more than 12 percent, with the rest coming from a wide variety of foodstuffs, spices, drugs, textiles, and miscellaneous goods. London, of course, was the most important port in English trade with the colonies, exporting four times the value of goods that went from the outports to the North American colonies, including 78 percent of English-manufactured exports and 88 percent of all reexports.

Under the Navigation Acts, the only legal colonial imports from Southern Europe were wine and salt. It has been said that such luxury goods as citrus and dried fruits, olives, anchovies, Ceylon hats, and Barcelona handkerchiefs also found their devious way into colonial hands; but in any case, the overall values of legal imports in this trade were quite small, averaging £68,000 annually in 1768–72. As we shall see in Chapter 5, this led to a healthy balance-of-payments surplus in the colonies' trade with Southern Europe.

Imports from the West Indies, on the other hand, were more numerous and of considerably greater magnitude. Average annual imports were £771,000 for the five-year period–more than ten times those from Southern Europe and 20 percent of all imports. Molasses, rum, and muscovado (brown, or semirefined, sugar) dominated this trade, accounting for more than three-quarters of the estimated

value of imports from the West Indies. The following lists
the value of some of the commodities of this trade in terms
of annual average values for 1768 through 1772:

Coffee	£15,000
Cotton	19,000
Molasses	199,000
Rum	278,000
Salt	30,000
Sugar	129,000
Wine	1,000

Most of the molasses (over 90 percent) went to New England
and the middle colonies, largely to be converted into rum in
the numerous distilleries (said to number sixty-three in Massachusetts in 1750 and about thirty in Rhode Island). Direct
imports of rum and of sugar were more evenly divided
among the various colonial regions, although the middle colonies took rather larger shares (perhaps indicating a regional
preference for West India rum as against the lower-quality
product from their New England neighbors). As to cotton,
somewhat more than 10 percent of that imported was reexported to Britain; most of that imported went to New England and the middle colonies. Other commodities imported
from the West Indies included cocoa, mahogany, sarsaparilla,
various dyewoods (such as logwood), and pimento.

The notorious slave trade furnished the most important
import from Africa (numbers and values of slaves are discussed in Chapter 5). Ivory, beeswax, and various types of
woods, such as ebony, were also imported, but in negligible
quantities compared to the total value of commodity imports.

The foregoing picture of trade has been based principally
upon evidence pertaining to the five-year period 1768–72.
Taking a longer view of the colonial period, what can we
discover about the relative (and changing) importance of
different routes of trade? The early-seventeenth-century focus, of course, was on direct trade with England. By the
middle of that century trades were beginning with the West
Indies and with Southern Europe, and by the end of the

colonial period these had grown to sizable proportions. From the fragmentary evidence of earlier years, it is impossible to determine the speed or the exact timing of the shifts. We can surmise, however, that the values were changing relative to direct trade with Britain throughout the eighteenth century, and, as we shall see in Chapter 9, this upswing for the West Indian trade continued after the American Revolution.

Though the discussion in this section is devoted largely to the overseas trade of the colonies, their commercial activity also included a lively interchange within and among themselves. Except to the extent that this was represented in the data for each colony's overseas trade, little can be said about internal market activities. What evidence we can find is fragmentary, for the most part. However, American customs records provide some figures on coastal shipping between the colonies that yield certain insights.[12]

This coastal trade served three basic functions: to distribute colonial products for local consumption, to collect commodities for export to overseas markets, and to distribute imports. For these latter purposes dockage and warehousing were provided by Boston, New York, Philadelphia, Charleston, and similar larger ports. The total values involved in coastal trade can probably never be computed because price information is simply not available for some of the commodities. However, from the American customs records the following computations of average relative values have been made for 1768–72:

	Exports	*Imports*
New England	£304,000	£289,000
Middle colonies	220,000	178,000
Upper South	88,000	73,000
Lower South	103,000	76,000
Total	£715,000	£616,000

These probably comprise the greatest part of the total value of the coastal trade (though imports from Britain that were reexported in the coastal trade were not included in the American customs records).[13] If so, then one can conclude that the coastal trade was at least one-quarter as valuable as colonial overseas trade, although it seems surprisingly small in comparison with total output. It was clearly most important to New England and the middle colonies. The New England colonies were in the business of importing large quantities of West Indian goods like rum and molasses and reexporting them or their derivatives, such as New England rum. The middle colonies also shared in this redistributive function.

The most valuable commodities imported into New England in the coastal trade were bread and, more importantly, flour. As a deficit region in cereals, New England imported largely from the middle colonies and perhaps, to a lesser extent, from the upper South. The southern staples of tobacco, indigo, rice, and naval stores appear to have been relatively unimportant in the coastal trade.

Thus if we are to assess the role of the coastal trade in colonial economic development, we see that the importance of the direct trade of the southern colonies with Great Britain is undiminished. Furthermore, the connection of New England and the middle colonies with the West Indies appears even more important. Consequently, despite its comparatively small volume, coastal trade played a helpful role in fostering overall colonial trade and commercial contacts. However, its most important role may have been in terms of social and political communication, drawing the scattered colonies together and fostering a growing sense of unity.

It is not within the scope of this book to elaborate upon the business framework within which this trade took place, nor upon the complex monetary system that had evolved by the late colonial period. These are long and involved stories.[14] It will suffice to say that, typically, small proprietorships or partnerships formed in the larger ports specialized in some aspect of the export and/or import business. In Virginia and Maryland, where large towns did not exist, local merchants sometimes handled the transactions, but often the plantation owner would sell his own tobacco and buy imported goods through an English merchant with whom he had a correspondent relationship. This arrangement was more typical of older tidewater areas, whereas in the more recently settled piedmont areas, a British firm (often a Scottish one from Glasgow) might maintain a representative called a factor to buy tobacco on site. Normally the factor also operated a store in which the tobacco grower would use the credit earned by his crop to purchase goods.

Money of all kinds was in circulation – coins brought in from the surpluses in trade with the West Indies and Southern Europe, along with the old Spanish dollar which was destined later to provide the model for the United States dollar. Most colonies had tried printing and issuing paper money, too, but this had met with varying degrees of success, and the money that did circulate was not adequate either in amount or in stability to satisfy completely the expanding needs of commerce and overseas trade of the colonies. Not until after the Revolution did uniform currency or commercial banks appear.

In such a situation, a large volume of credit transactions was inevitable. The resultant elaborate structure of debt took the form of book credits (accounts receivable and payable), bonds, and "money placed at interest" with particular individuals. Colonial merchants in the seaport cities usually purchased imported goods on one year's credit from British merchants or manufacturers. These goods would in turn be sold on credit to other merchants, often in small towns or the country, or to peddlers, or at retail directly to consumers. The merchant might be paid in all manner of ways, for example, with goods produced by his customers, or by services rendered by them. Most debts would be paid, although some became uncollectible even as today. The successful merchant, however, would gradually accumulate larger and larger balances owed by his customers. Such debt itself would often serve as money when the merchant, acting as a private banker, would transfer the debt (or credit) on his books from one individual to another. These magnitudes undoubtedly became large; and upon this complex credit structure many (probably most) market transactions took place during the colonial period.

Patterns of shipping and trade

Now, with the eye of a mapmaker, let us take a final look at the patterns of trade and shipping that developed during the whole colonial period. Traditional descriptions of the trades of that time correctly show a direct, shuttle-type traffic with Great Britain; but with respect to other areas, the literature deals largely with the alleged "triangles of trade," of which the most famous is the one between New England and Africa. In this case rum and trinkets are said to have been exchanged for slaves, who were then taken across the "middle passage" to the West Indies, where they were traded for sugar, molasses, specie, and bills of exchange; the final leg of the triangle brought these goods back to New England, where the molasses was manufactured into rum to begin another cycle.

A second triangle was the shipment of foodstuffs and wood products from the middle colonies or New England to the West Indies, where they were traded for sugar and other tropical and semitropical goods; these were taken to England and sold to buy manufactures as cargo for the return voyage (unless the ship itself were to be sold in England). Yet another triangle took a ship carrying fish, wheat, and wood products to Southern Europe, where the cargo was exchanged for wine, salt, fruit, and cash; thence to England to exchange these for manufactures to be returned to the colonies.

The New England shipper is frequently portrayed as a jack-of-all-trades who engaged in a "peddling and huckstering business, involving an enormous amount of petty detail, frequent exchanges, and a constant lading and unlading as the captains and masters moved from port to port."[15] One contemporary observer, Benjamin Franklin, speaking to a Parliamentary committee in 1766, mentioned the "circuitous voyages" of Pennsylvania merchants.[16]

Actually, this traditional view of the shipping activity of New England and the middle colonies is totally inaccurate both in emphasis and in fact. For instance, of the annual average of 107,285 tons that cleared New England between 1768 and 1772, only 1,023 tons were destined for Africa— less than 1 percent of the total. This route was even less significant to the middle colonies. Therefore, as we saw in the discussion of the *values* of overseas trade, it appears that the traditional preoccupation with the African slave trade has again distorted the relative importance of the trade route itself.

It is equally evident that comparatively few colonial vessels were engaged in triangular runs, as regards either the middle colonies or New England in their respective trades with the West Indies and Great Britain. Of hundreds of vessels that have been traced from both colonial areas en route to Barbados and Jamaica and outward from these islands, only a few departed to Great Britain.

As to the third triangular route (New England or the middle colonies to Southern Europe, thence to Britain, and home), necessary evidence is lacking to prove or disprove its existence. We do know, however, that in the trade of both colonial areas with Southern Europe, we find a remarkable similarity between the tonnages of ships clearing from colonial ports and ships reentering those ports: an indication, at least, that two-way direct trade prevailed. In short, while some colonial shippers undoubtedly followed multilateral routes and route switching, it appears that the traditional emphasis on triangular trades is misplaced.

The relative costs of providing market and shipping services primarily determined the ownership of vessels in the various trade routes. In general, ships trading between Great Britain and the southern colonies or the West Indies were British. For intercolonial trade, and between the colo-

nies and most overseas areas other than Britain itself, colonial-owned ships predominated.[17] Regardless of ownership,
high costs attached to every sailing: over and above the natural hazards of the voyage were the difficulties of acquiring
information about changing market conditions, and the relatively great expense of manning the ships. These factors also
influenced the types of business arrangements governing the
voyages: frequently a single merchant would undertake both
the marketing and the shipping of goods, instead of considering them separate operations as we do today. Curtis
Nettels states:

> The freighting and marketing of goods in those days
> were simply aspects of a single operation, and freights
> and profits were frequently indistinguishable. Often a
> merchant owner shipped his goods in his own vessel.
> Other trades dispatched consignments to designated
> ports, paying the freight to the owner. By a third
> method, a group of merchants chartered a vessel, in
> whole or in part, paying a monthly charge determined
> by the space hired rather than by the quantity of the
> goods shipped and the length of the voyage.[18]

Marketing was usually accomplished by consigning the
goods either to a ship's captain who would act for the merchant in selling, trading, and buying commodities, or to a
factor who would handle the transactions in his local market.
Since the merchant was wholly dependent on his agent, a
good deal of trust (and risk) was involved. It is not surprising that colonial merchants tended to favor homegrown
ships and captains: the friendlier the relations between merchant and agent, and the greater their speed of communication, the lower the risk that vitally affected the costs of trade
over various routes.

Nearness to market was another crucial consideration because both communication and transportation were fairly
primitive. In the tobacco trade, for example, New England
shippers labored under the disadvantage of distance: it was

more costly for them than the British to coordinate information on the changing conditions of the tobacco markets either in Europe (the buyer) or in the southern colonies (the seller) in that two-way trade. On the other hand, colonial shippers and merchants enjoyed a comparable advantage over the British in the West Indies trade. They could respond more quickly to market fluctuations, and thus their risks, as well as their costs of information, were lower.[19]

Layover time in ports was the cause of still another differential in shipping costs. It was customary for crews to remain on board while ships were loading or unloading cargo anywhere except in home ports (where they were discharged).[20] Labor was relatively costly, and wages mounted rapidly during this lost time. In the tobacco trade, British shippers had to pay these layover wages in colonial ports, but colonial shippers (except those actually resident in southern port cities) were doubly burdened by having to pay layover wages both in the Chesapeake loading areas and in the British port of destination. Between home ports and the Caribbean, on the other hand, the colonial shippers had the advantage.

The matter of layover wages also helps to explain why specialized routes and shuttle patterns came to be favored over multilateral or triangular patterns of trade. These complex, many-port routes would otherwise have offered definite advantages: it is clearly desirable for a ship to carry as full a cargo as possible, and in the West Indies trade, for example, it would have seemed intelligent for a ship's captain, typically acting as agent for his shipper, to visit many different ports, picking up and discharging commodities as he went and always seeking the best markets for his particular cargoes. But now consider the matter in the light of layover time and wage bills. In such loosely organized trade, it would have needed several trips among the islands simply to learn the ropes, to meet the buyers, and to agree on the terms of any transaction. Where many media of exchange were in circulation it was difficult or impossible to determine exact prices; and when a transaction involved barter, the process could go on endlessly, with wage bills steadily mounting. Such lengthy port times offset any gains from the trade; moreover, even where credit facilities might have been available, the risks of long-distance default were great.

Given these many problems, it is not surprising that most colonial shippers chose to follow well-established sea routes between a limited number of ports.[21] As a result, by the end of the colonial period a highly specialized and sophisticated commerce had come into being in the thirteen colonies, centering in a resident mercantile sector in the towns of New England and the middle colonies. As part of the larger Atlantic economy of its time, this prosperous trade bolstered the colonial balance of payments and supported colonial economic development in general, as we shall see in the following chapters.

Glossary of terms

Balance of trade
    The balance of trade is that part of a nation's balance of payments that deals with commodity imports and commodity exports (see glossary, Chapter 1). The "balance" specifically means the difference between the value of commodity exports and the value of commodity imports. A "favorable" balance of trade occurs when the value of commodity exports is greater than the value of commodity imports. An "unfavorable" balance of trade exists when the value of commodity imports is greater than the value of commodity exports.

Macroeconomic analysis
    That part of economic theory whose purpose is the explanation of the behavior of the overall economy, and broad sectors of it (such as the household sector, the business sector, the government and the foreign sector). It deals with such questions as: What determines the level of output? Why does unemployment exist? What causes inflation?

Selected readings

Brock, Leslie V., *The Currency of the American Colonies, 1700–1764* (New York: Arno Press, 1975).

Bruckey, Stuart (ed.), *The Colonial Merchant: Sources and Readings* (New York: Harcourt Brace Jovanovich, 1966).

Coleman, D. C. (ed.), *Revisions in Mercantilism* (London: Methuen, 1969).

Ernst, Joseph A., *Money and Politics in America, 1755–1775* (Chapel Hill, N.C.: University of North Carolina Press, 1973).

Minchinton, W. E. (ed.), *The Growth of English Overseas Trade in the 17th and 18th Centuries* (London: Methuen, 1969).

Nettels, Curtis P., *The Money Supply of the American Colonies before 1720* (Madison, Wis.: University of Wisconsin Studies in the Social Sciences and History, No. 20, October 1934; rpt. New York: Augustus M. Kelley, 1964).

Shepherd, James F., and Gary M. Walton, *Shipping, Maritime Trade, and the Economic Development of Colonial North America* (Cambridge: Cambridge University Press, 1972), Chapters 3, 4, and 6.

Shepherd, James F., and Samuel H. Williamson, "The Coastal Trade of the British North American Colonies, 1768–1772," *Journal of Economic History,* XXXII, 4 (December 1972), pp. 783–810.

5

Overseas trade and capital flows

Few issues were of keener interest to economic policy makers within the empire than the question of trade balances. Indeed, as stated in Chapter 4, the cornerstone of seventeenth- and eighteenth-century mercantilist doctrine rested on the belief that it is economically advantageous for a nation to export more than it imports – that is, to have favorable balances of trade. This usually resulted in an inflow of precious metals from other areas. To many, a growing hoard of gold and silver was synonymous with rising national wealth.

Over the years the Crown implemented a variety of measures to curb imports and develop industries that would lead to import substitution throughout the empire. The development of war-related manufactures was heavily stressed, together with complementary activities such as shipbuilding and the provision of merchant shipping services. Moreover, one of the primary motives for British expansion throughout North America was the desire to attain greater economic self-sufficiency within the empire. As a means toward economic independence, commerce with the colonies was viewed as superior to trade with other nation-states (or their colonies), where a breakdown resulting either from war or from adverse changes in trade policies could lead to critical supply shortages.

The concern with trade balances was not limited merely to the European shores of the empire. Because of the colonists' nearly insatiable desires for European manufactures, they persistently faced difficulties in paying for these imports;

particularly troublesome, especially after 1750, were the chronic deficits arising in trade with England. In reply to a question asked by a parliamentary committee in 1760 on how Pennsylvania paid for its trade deficit with Great Britain, Benjamin Franklin responded:

> The balance is paid by our produce carried to the West Indies, and sold in our own islands, or to the French, Spaniards, Danes, and Dutch; by the same carried to other colonies in North-America, as to New-England, Nova-Scotia, Newfoundland, Carolina and Georgia, by the same carried to different parts of Europe, as Spain, Portugal and Italy: In all which places we receive either money, bills of exchange, or commodities that suit for remittance to Britain; which together with all the profits on the industry of our merchants and mariners, arising in those circuitous voyages, and the freights made by their ships, center finally in Britain, to discharge the balance, and pay for British manufactures continually used in the province, or sold to foreigners by our traders.[1]

As shown in Table 7, the American colonies' balance of trade with England registered a large deficit in the eighteenth century. We shall see below that this was due mainly to the demands of the New England and the middle colonies, but even the southern colonies appear to have incurred small deficits in their commodity trade with the mother country.

As emphasized by Franklin, the *trade deficits* to Britain could be paid by surpluses earned in trades to other overseas areas, supplemented by earnings from shipping and other mercantile services. Other sources of *foreign exchange,* such as expenditures by the British defense forces stationed in the colonies, augmented the sterling inflow.

To determine the relative importance of these and other sources of *exchange earnings* (and expenditures), we need to portray quantitatively the various components of a balance of payments for the colonies. Such a task is tedious but extremely useful. More is at stake than the mere question of how the trade deficits with Great Britain were paid. Of vital concern to the colonists was the problem of chronic money shortages in the colonies. Were the trade deficits with Britain offset by surpluses in other trades or by exchange earnings? Did trade cause a persistent specie drain from the colonies? Alternatively, were the trade deficits financed through *capital inflows;* that is, by growing indebtedness in the colonies to British creditors? Were these capital inflows critical to the economic development of the colonies, and did they take on the form of "foreign aid," signifying extensive subsidization of colonial development? Lastly, there remains a captivating question: Was growing indebtedness a possible motivation for revolt? Many historians have cited the growing indebtedness of southern planters to London merchants who handled their tobacco, hinting perhaps that the planters were exploited and economically mesmerized by London credit monopolists. Analysis of the southern regions' deficits or surpluses in their balance of payments in the late colonial period yields important evidence on this issue.

Table 7. *Commodity trade between England and the American colonies (thousands of £)*

Years	Annual average exports	Annual average imports	Annual average deficit
1721–30	442	509	67
1731–40	559	698	139
1741–50	599	923	324
1751–60	808	1,704	896
1761–70	1,203	1,942	739

Source: J. F. Shepherd and G. M. Walton, *Shipping, Maritime Trade and the Economic Development of Colonial North America* (Cambridge: Cambridge University Press, 1972), p. 42.

A balance of payments, 1768–72

To begin our investigation of a balance of payments for the American colonies in the late colonial period we first need to account for the final balances in commodity trade with the various overseas areas. Table 8, displaying a breakdown of these trade balances for major regions, confirms the view in Table 7 that deficits with Great Britain, especially for New England and the middle colonies, were significant in the late colonial period. Partially offsetting surpluses were earned in the commodity trades with Southern Europe (and to a very minor degree with Africa also), but commodity trade with the West Indies was slightly "unfavorable" from the perspective of the mainland colonies.

The most important source of foreign exchange earnings to offset the overall deficits in commodity trade was the sale

Table 8. *Average annual commodity trade balances of the 13 colonies, 1768–72 (thousands of £)*

	Great Britain and Ireland	Southern Europe	West Indies	Africa	All trades
New England	−609	+48	−36	+19	−577
Middle colonies	−786	+153	−10	+1	−643
Upper South	−50	+90	−9	0	+30
Lower South	−23	+48	+44	*	+69
Total colonies	−1,468	+339	−11	+20	−1,121

Notes: A plus sign (+) signifies a surplus, with exports exceeding imports in value. A minus sign (−) denotes a deficit. (*) denotes amounts less than £500. Regional balances may not add to totals as a result of rounding.

Values are expressed in prices in the mainland colonies. Therefore import values include shipping costs, commissions, and other handling costs. Export values do not include these distribution costs.
Source: J. F. Shepherd and G. M. Walton, *Shipping, Maritime Trade and the Economic Development of Colonial North America* (Cambridge: Cambridge University Press, 1972), p. 115.

of shipping services plus such "invisible" related earnings as insurance and mercantile profits. Colonial shipping proceeds amounted to approximately £600,000 per year in the late colonial period. Probably more than £200,000 annually was earned by colonial merchants through insurance charges and commissions. Together these "invisible" earnings offset more than 60 percent of the overall trade deficit. Most of these earnings – more than 80 percent – went into the pockets of residents of New England and the middle colonies. This fact cannot be stressed too much. Only the mercantile activities of New Englanders and middle colonists, especially in the West Indian trade, enabled them to bring in large quantities of imports from Great Britain, since these colonies lacked the exportable commodity staples of the southern colonies. For all thirteen colonies together, earnings from such activities exceeded the return from tobacco – the single most important commodity export. Further, these activities strengthened the vigorous mercantile sector so important to later development.

Another aspect of seafaring economics, the sale of ships, largely to Great Britain, became a persistent credit item in the colonies' balance of payments. Recently, Jacob Price has suggested that this item averaged at least £140,000 annually from 1763 to 1775.[2] Again, the lion's share of these earnings went to New England, with the middle colonies receiving some smaller portion.

Table 9 shows the effects of all these shipping-related items for the thirteen colonies as a whole. From an overall deficit of £1,120,000 in the balance of commodity trade, ship sales and "invisible" earnings together reduced the negative balance on current account to only £160,000.

One significant item on the deficit side, for the colonies, was the outpouring of funds to foreign markets for the trade in human beings. Not only slaves but indentured servants were brought in by the shipload. Estimates place the per-capita cost for an indentured servant at approximately £10; thus for the 5,000 to 10,000 indentured servants who

Table 9. *A balance of payments for the 13 colonies (average yearly exchanges, 1768–72, in thousands of £)*[a]

	Debit	Credit
Commodities		
Exports[b]		2,800
Imports[c]	3,920	
Balance of trade	1,120	
Ship sales		140
Invisible earnings		
Shipping earnings		600
Merchant commissions, risk, and insurance		220
Balance on current account from trade	160	
Payments for human beings		
Indentured servants	80	
Slaves	200	
British collections and expenditures in colonies		
Taxes and duties	40	
Salaries of British civil servants		40
Military expenditures		230
Naval expenditures		170
Capital and monetary flows		
Specie ⎫		40
Indebtedness ⎭		

Notes: [a] All calculations are rounded to the nearest 1,000. Note that the figures in this table differ somewhat from those given in the source (Shepherd and Walton, 1972). Because Newfoundland, Quebec, Nova Scotia, Florida, Bermuda, and the Bahamas were included in the source but excluded here, the primary aggregate estimates of exports, imports and shipping earnings have been adjusted downward by £210,000, £420,000, and £10,000, respectively.
[b] Exports are valued F.O.B. exclusive of ocean transport costs and other merchandising costs.
[c] Imports are valued C.I.F., that is, including ocean transportation costs, insurance, interest, and commission charges.
Source: J. F. Shepherd and G. M. Walton, *Shipping, Maritime Trade and the Economic Development of Colonial North America* (Cambridge: Cambridge University Press, 1972), Chapters 6, 7, and 8.

arrived annually during the late colonial period, a mid-range estimate of total cost would approximate £80,000 per year, as shown in Table 9. By far the majority of such servants went to Pennsylvania, Maryland, and Virginia.

Most slaves imported into the colonies went to the South, fewer than 10 percent being sold or ultimately located north of the Chesapeake. The rapidly expanding lower South took nearly three out of every four slaves sold in the southern area in the late colonial period. For the colonies as a whole, the average annual debit due to slave purchases amounted to approximately £200,000, as payments per slave averaged between £35 and £40 for the slightly more than 5,000 slaves sold per year in the late colonial period.

Expenditures made by the British government in the colonies went far toward offsetting the remaining deficits in the colonists' current account. Defense was undoubtedly the most costly item, but Great Britain also carried the financial load of civil administration and justice, and of administering and enforcing customs regulations. These costs to Great Britain cannot be accurately determined, but in any case they are irrelevant to this study. Rather, our concern is with how much British currency went into the purchase of goods and services in the colonies and, on the other side of the scale, how much colonial revenue was extracted by the British government, primarily by way of customs duties. From the available evidence, it seems almost certain that the cost of civil and customs administration exceeded the gain from customs revenues, which averaged almost £40,000 per annum for the period 1768–72; but as presented in Table 9 we have conservatively estimated the costs of collection and administration as merely equaling the revenues collected.[3]

In contrast to expenditures for civil government and customs administration, it is probable that British military and naval costs resulted in significant earnings of sterling for the colonies. The standing British army during this period consisted of sixteen regiments; at full strength, each regiment numbered 477 men, but it is likely that desertions, illness, and casualties kept the total lower. General Gage's report of July 19, 1775, lists the strength of each regiment as varying from 333 to 457 men each. At full strength, the pay and subsistence for a regiment came to almost £18,000 per year, or over £230,000 per year for sixteen regiments at about 80 percent of strength. Undoubtedly, almost all of this pay and subsistence was spent in the colonies.

The Royal Navy's North American squadron ranged around twenty-seven vessels of various sizes during this period; had they been manned by the full complement of men and officers (probably over 4,000) the wages and subsistence would have approximated £260,000. Granted, it is probable that many vessels were undermanned and, in any case, that sailors had less opportunity than soldiers to spend their wages ashore. It is thus impossible to say with certainty how much navy pay poured into colonial tills, but it seems reasonable to guess that at least £150,000 to £200,000 ended that way. Our figure in Table 9 is £170,000.

In all, then, it appears that British defense expenditures in the colonies must have reached an annual £400,000 by the eve of the Revolution. This figure seems relatively conservative, representing as it does only about 10 percent of the annual peacetime defense costs of the entire British establishment in the years 1773–5 – a total of £3,811,000.[4] If the foregoing estimates are close to the mark, even this conservatively set inflow of funds to the colonies would have reduced the deficit in the colonial balance of payments to a relatively insignificant £40,000 per year.

Monetary flows, capital flows, and debt

The remaining small deficit in the colonies' balance of payments–thus estimated at around £40,000 annually in the late colonial period – necessarily would have had to be paid by specie or bullion, or with colonial IOU's, or with some combination of both. No significant part could have been paid with precious metals, because the mainland colonies lacked any domestic sources for these. Bullion and specie earned in the surplus trades with Southern Europe and the West Indies and from British governmental and defense expenditures in the colonies primarily settled the trade deficits with England. Various kinds of coin were in circulation, together with *bills of exchange,* earned in the West Indian trade, which served as a form of paper money in colonial trade.

Until the mining and minting of gold and silver (which had to await a later period of settlement in the Southwest), the colonists of North America faced a distressing and unsustainable net outflow of specie and bullion. The continual drain of coin in trade with Britain, coupled with the issuance of uncertain paper money by various colonies, caused loud complaints about the lack of any stable money supply. In the absence of commercial banks or the firm hand of a national government which might have created a stable monetary system (as later occurred following the adoption of the Constitution), an adequate supply of money in colonial America could have been based only upon a bountiful stock of specie – coins valuable in themselves for their metal content. The colonists, however, chose not to accumulate such a domestic money supply, but rather to spend such gold and silver as they earned from trade to import British manufactured goods so desirable to a developing economy.

Historians generally have interpreted these complaints about monetary distress as meaning that the colonies had balance-of-payments deficits. Such conclusions, although justified, do not necessarily imply that the deficits were large. The use of coin and other monetary media to pay for deficits in the trade with England was simply a way of transferring the surpluses earned in the West Indian and Southern European trades. Such a monetary drain would have occurred even had colonial trade been perfectly balanced with no deficits or surpluses: only if balance-of-payments surpluses consistently had been earned would the colonies have accumulated an adequate supply of circulating coin. We are justified in assuming that balance-of-payments surpluses did not occur, since no such supply did accumulate. However, the monetary drain and the complaints of monetary distress would be perfectly consistent with even the small balance-of-payments deficit estimated above.

To the extent that any deficit remained on the colonies' current account, therefore, it could not have been settled with specie or bullion; rather it was increasingly financed by short-term credit which, underwriting the growing trade between Britain and the colonies, was of crucial importance to the commerce of the eighteenth century. Production and distribution must be financed at all levels, from the first purchase of raw materials until the final good reaches the consumer. In the trade between Britain and the colonies, an American merchant typically bought goods from a British merchant or manufacturer on a year-long credit, the cost of which was included in the price of the goods. An alternative arrangement was common in Virginia: a Scottish firm would set up its representative in the colonies as a storekeeper, stocking his store with goods that could be either sold or traded for tobacco or other American products. In each case, the short-term credit that financed British imports was furnished by British mercantile firms.

Because new orders for goods were continually being sent to Britain, even while previous purchases were being paid for, large trade credits were continually in flux. Although some debts undoubtedly were not paid within the year's time and might therefore be considered longer-term loans, the bulk of this mercantile debt represented short-term trade credit – that is to say, real capital inflows to the American colonies – in the sense that the balance of payments was affected by the increasing American indebtedness to residents of Britain.

These capital inflows were not directed toward long-term investment in the colonies, and British merchants themselves probably held few claims on such investments; yet it is only fair to note that because this credit was furnished by the British, colonial savings were freed for exactly that purpose:

to make long-term investments in land improvement, roads, and such capital installations as ships, warehouses, and public buildings. For purposes of colonial development, the British short-term credits represented a helping hand, their form being less important than their amount.

Some historians, strongly emphasizing the growing short-term indebtedness of the colonists to British merchants in the late colonial period, have maintained that southern tobacco planters in particular were falling into a disastrous relationship with London tobacco merchants. Once into debt and thus economically bound, they were exploited by being charged high prices for goods and high interest rates on debt. It has even been argued that planters in these straits had strong incentives to support the Revolution.

But was there actually such widespread and growing indebtedness in the southern regions? Looking at Table 8, we can now add invisible earnings and ship sales to the figures shown for the total deficits on commodity trade to all overseas markets for each colonial region. This calculation gives the following yearly regional deficits (−) or surpluses (+).[5]

New England	−£50,000
Middle colonies	−£350,000
Southern colonies	+£240,000

Thus the major deficit regions were north of the Chesapeake, and debts appear to have been piling up primarily in the middle colonies. The southern regions were favored with more than enough surplus in their current accounts to pay for purchases of slaves and indentured servants.

Although we lack a precise division of the surplus between the two southern regions (see note 5), at least half (and probably more) of the £240,000 accrued to the upper South. If as much as one-fourth of the indentured servants and slaves went there, this would leave £50,000 in surplus after these purchases: (£120,000 − £20,000 − £50,000 = £50,000). Since British expenditures for defense in the upper South brought in additional exchange, there can be little doubt

that the region, and indeed all the southern colonies, suffered no growing indebtedness or specie drain in the late
colonial period.[6]

Despite these trade balances, however, following the Revolution British merchants submitted to the British government (in February 1791) a claim that slightly less than £5
million was due them from Americans.[7] These claims, shown
in Table 10, Column 1, include fourteen years of accumulated interest. Assuming that this interest was calculated at a
rate of 5 percent,[8] compounded annually, the claims for
debt as of 1776 would indicate the amounts shown in Column 2; the figures should be viewed cautiously, however, as
they are probably grossly exaggerated. Aubrey Land argues
that the figures were magnified by as much as 800 percent;
the Americans, in fact, honored only one-eighth of the
claims by the British.[9] For another thing, some debts out-

Table 10. *British merchants claims of debt owed them by Americans
in 1791*

Colony	(1) 1791	(2) 1776
Virginia	£2,305,409	£1,164,000
South Carolina	687,954	347,000
Maryland	571,455	289,000
North Carolina	379,344	192,000
Massachusetts	287,983	145,000
Georgia	247,782	125,000
Pennsylvania	229,452	116,000
New York	175,095	88,000
Rhode Island	49,208	25,000
Connecticut	28,653	14,000
New Hampshire	21,796	11,000
New Jersey	524	—
Totals	£4,984,655	£2,516,000

Source: J. F. Shepherd and G. M. Walton, *Shipping, Maritime Trade
and the Economic Development of Colonial North America* (Cambridge:
Cambridge University Press, 1972), p. 132.

standing in 1776 were undoubtedly paid between 1776 and
1790, generally from the large commercial towns in the
more northern colonies, thus explaining why the bulk of the
alleged debt left in 1790 was owed by the southern colonies.
For good reason, fewer debts would have been collected
there: the distribution of British goods in the South was
typically handled by partners or agents of British firms.
Under normal conditions, these representatives would extend credit to the planters against the harvest as collateral;
when that came in, the debts were paid with produce that
the merchant shipped to England. With the outbreak of the
Revolution, that picture predictably changed. The agents
promptly left America before harvest time and the debts (of
moderate amounts but great numbers) remained outstand-
ing. Thus the claims expressed in Table 10 do not represent
any increasing indebtedness in the plantation areas. Nor, as
part of the normal short-term credit cycle on the eve of the
Revolution, would they have motivated the planters to seek
an escape through revolt. The point is that credit normally
given against the collateral of the harvest was still outstand-
ing in 1776 (and in 1790) because the agents or partners of
British firms doing business in the South found it convenient to either leave the business, or leave for home, before
the harvest came in.

Consequently, there were debts owed to British merchants
by Southerners in 1776. However, growing indebtedness in
the southern regions was not widespread on the eve of the
Revolution, and southern ambitions to escape debts to the
British could not have been a primary motivation for revolt.

The longer view

The foregoing conclusions are based on evidence largely
from the years 1768–72, and skeptics certainly may doubt
the validity of so few years as accurately representing the
longer view. Although the average trade figures and other

calculations presented do not apply to any specific year, they probably are reasonably indicative of the late colonial period between the ending of the Seven Years' War in 1763 and the outbreak of revolt in 1775. For that span, these figures currently stand as our most systematic available summary of the colonies' external economic relations and the average movements of exchange resulting from trade and other economic relationships.

War years are of course another matter, and there were many in the eighteenth century. It may not be valid to extend our generalizations to them, for it is a truism to say that war changes everything in the economic picture. For one thing, during periods of conflict British merchants would have been unlikely either to make long-term investments so far from home or to allow short-term mercantile debt to rise substantially. In regard to the balance of payments: if the official values of British exports and imports to and from the colonies can be accepted as a rough guide, it would appear that Britain's exports gained substantially as a percentage of the value of trade during the Seven Years' War (see Figure 8). However, it is probable that this economic advantage to England was offset by the greater need for defense costs in the colonies during the period.[10]

Even when relative calm settled over the international scene, the sterling spent for defending (as well as for administering) the colonies may well have constituted a significant percentage of total trade over most of the eighteenth century. Although the British standing army in the colonies was considerably smaller during the first half of that century than it later became, there is no indication that naval forces were any less powerful. Indeed, the official values suggest that total military expenditures made an important contribution to the relatively good colonial balance of payments with England during the earlier years; Nettels states that Britain spent £414,000 on the defense of commerce and the coast of the mainland colonies in the four war years, 1708–11.[11]

After 1745, the deficits to England increased, but they were in part counterbalanced by improving trade with two other partners. First, as shown in Figure 8, the trade with Scotland showed an average surplus of about £45,000 annually from 1755 through 1760.[12] Second, surpluses also resulted from an expanding commerce with Southern Europe and the West Indies during these decades.

In summary, then, we conclude that either no deficits, or small ones, marked the current accounts of the colonies during the eighteenth century and up to the Revolution. It appears that by the beginning of the eighteenth century the colonies had already become economically self-sufficient, with the colonial goods complementing those produced in the mother country so that both stood to gain from the trade. The short-term loans from British merchants that financed trade had to be repaid and were primarily a device to ease the transactions; nor does British long-term investment in the colonies appear to have been significant after 1700.

With the highly important exception of defense, the colo-

Figure 8. Exports and imports of the thirteen colonies to and from England, 1700–70, and Scotland, 1755–70 (official values). *Source: Historical Statistics of the United States, Colonial Times to 1957* (Washington D.C.: Government Printing Office, 1960), p. 757, and Customs 14, Public Record Office, London.

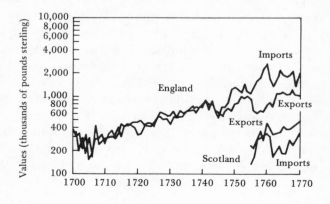

nies were thus apparently not subsidized by Britain to any great extent. The formation of capital in the New World depended almost exclusively on the steady accretion of savings and investment from the pockets of the colonists themselves. It cannot be determined precisely how much was saved and invested annually by the 2.1 million residents in the late colonial period. According to our estimates, which will be elaborated in Chapter 7, incomes probably averaged in the neighborhood of £12 per person. If each saved as little as £1 of this (and 8 percent is a low expected rate of saving from gross income), then total capital accumulation per year would have exceeded £2 million. Thus the estimated capital inflow from Britain – which we noted earlier in this chapter as averaging less than £50,000 per year – would not have provided 5 percent of domestic capital formation.

Only when we consider the costs to Britain of the civil government and defense of the colonies does her role in contributing to their economic development take on truly impressive dimensions. The young nation was quickly to learn, after independence was won, the real financial burden of self-protection in a hostile world.

Glossary of terms

Trade deficits
   Trade deficits occur in trade with another area or country when payments for imports exceed earnings from exports to that area or country. Such deficits must be paid from surpluses (earnings greater than payments) earned in other areas, or by borrowing, or by payment from accumulations of specie or bullion.

Foreign exchange
   Foreign exchange is the money of foreign nations obtained from selling goods or services to those nations. The importance of foreign-exchange earnings is that they can be used to buy goods and services produced in other nations (imports).

Exchange earnings
   Earnings of foreign exchange.

Capital inflows
   Capital inflows represent loans or direct investment from foreign

investors, such as a resident of Britain. They may be short-term or long-term loans, or direct investment in an American firm or piece of land.

Bills of exchange

Documents used in commerce and finance dealing with the shipment of goods and the collection of debts. The seller of goods would draw up a bill stating that the buyer would pay a certain sum on a certain date, and send it to the buyer, who would write "accepted" on it and endorse it with his or her signature. Because it then became a promise to pay on the part of the buyer, it became valuable and often served as paper currency, passing from the hands of one person to another until it ended up back in the country of origin, where the buyer would arrange payment. Its importance was that it facilitated trade and the movement of funds from areas of trade surpluses to areas of trade deficits.

Selected readings

Nettels, Curtis P., *The Money Supply of the American Colonies before 1720* (Madison, Wis.: University of Wisconsin Studies in the Social Sciences and History, No. 20, October 1934; rpt. New York: Augustus M. Kelley, 1964).

Price, Jacob M., "A Note on the Value of Colonial Exports of Shipping," *Journal of Economic History*, XXXVI, 3 (September 1976), pp. 704–24.

Shepherd, James F., and Gary M. Walton, *Shipping, Maritime Trade, and the Economic Development of Colonial North America* (Cambridge: Cambridge University Press, 1972), Chapters 7, 8.

6

Productivity and economic progress

Economic progress in the colonial period stemmed from growth in the stock of land, labor, and capital, broadly defined, and from increases in productivity. Both historically and currently, economic progress, as measured in terms of rises in per-capita income or wealth, has stemmed primarily from the latter, that is, from human efforts that enlarged output relative to the inputs of land, labor, and capital. To understand the unique historical circumstances surrounding these gains requires an investigation of the rates and causes of advance in productivity in the major economic sectors and industries.

Before advancing to the empirical evidence and historical setting, it is useful to distinguish and elaborate on three general sources of productivity change: (1) technological change, (2) improved human skills and abilities, (3) improvements in economic organization.

We view *technological change* as an advance in knowledge that permits a smaller number of inputs to produce a given amount of output. This should be distinguished conceptually from *technical diffusion,* which involves the spread of a particular technology. The two frequently operate closely together, but as we shall see, sometimes there are substantial delays in technical diffusion because of restrictive barriers. Moreover, it must be remembered that the use of different techniques in different places may not always mean that one place is using more advanced techniques than another. These differences may be due to differences in the relative

113

prices of resources between the areas. Granted that some substitution of inputs in the production process is possible, there will be an incentive to use more of the relatively cheaper inputs and less of the relatively expensive ones to produce some given level of output. For example, in the colonies, land was relatively cheaper and labor relatively more expensive than in England. Colonists often farmed around tree stumps, did less to retard depletion of their land (by such things as fertilization), and followed other practices that used relatively less labor and capital than did farmers in England. This did not reflect different technologies of farming, but rather differences in the relative prices of labor, capital, and land.

The degree of skills and abilities embodied in the labor force may be determined by such things as the amount of formal education each member of the labor force has acquired, the skills acquired from experience, on-the-job training, levels of nutrition and health, and so forth. These *investments in human capital* contribute to the special skills needed to adapt and modify techniques, the quality of labor required for their widespread use, and the many professional and other skills demanded in society. Formal education did not generally play a vital role in the process of colonial life. Learning from experience and apprenticeship programs (often in the form of indentured servitude) and on-the-job training were the main forms of investment in human capital. It seems clear that the accumulation of practical experience over time did mean in increase in such investments during the colonial period.

Improvements in economic organization can raise productivity in a variety of ways. In particular, an important aspect of colonial economic development was the increasing regional specialization made possible through greater exchange and trade, especially for overseas markets. This may have involved a greater division of labor, such as the separating of tasks as envisaged by Adam Smith, but probably a better description of this increased regional specialization was that, as time passed, more people simply turned their activities toward producing certain commodities or services for markets. These types of production were those in which the colonists held a comparative advantage and thus received a greater remuneration.

An important characteristic of the American people from the period of first settlement has been their motivation and responsiveness to economic opportunities. This has resulted not only in a greater degree of labor and capital mobility than existed in Europe, but also a willingness to accept changes in economic organization, even when such changes sometimes proved harmful to particular groups or individuals.

Distribution costs

As emphasized earlier, a primary factor in the development of this frontier economy was the growth of trade and the rise of a domestic commercial sector. It is important to keep in mind that in the economic sense markets in that age functioned imperfectly. Prices among regions fluctuated much more than can be explained by differences in costs and, as Bell notes with respect to the West Indian trade, "Thanks to the smallness of the islands and their extreme dependence on outside supplies, any kind of American produce was apt to command very different prices in any two of them at the same time. For the same reasons prices fell and rose sharply with the arrival of fresh consignments or the nonappearance of those expected."[1]

Supply responses to market changes eventually improved as the volume of trade grew and as problems of market uncertainties, slow communications, and incomplete information were gradually overcome. Such barriers, or "natural tariffs," which tended to limit trade and to encourage subsistence activities, presented substantial obstacles throughout the colonial period, however. For instance, Table 11 shows the numerous explicit charges imposed on pitch, a fairly common colonial export, just before the Revolution.

These various impediments to distribution loomed large in the total costs of bulky, low-valued products, but even in the case of relatively expensive light goods they formed a significant part of the total costs to consumers. For instance, high-value English manufactures generally sold for as much as 80 to 140 percent more in the colonies than in England in the early eighteenth century, and no doubt had commanded an even greater premium in earlier years. Such markups did not persist, however. By 1750, prices on British wares ranged from 45 to 75 percent higher in the colonies than in

Table 11. *Accounts of sales, charges, and net proceeds on 252 barrels of pitch in London, 1775*

	£	s.	d.
Gross sales	203	9	6
Freight	71	17	6
Primage	2	1	8
Pierage	1	3	5
Duty	11	9	0
Sufferance and duplicate	0	3	6
Landwaiters and weighters	1	10	0
Oath	0	1	0
Weighers and henekens	0	2	0
Post entry on two barrels	0	3	0
Land Surveyors for certificate	1	5	0
Passing certificate in the custom house	1	1	0
Clerk at the Navy office	0	2	6
Heneken for wharfage	4	4	0
¼ discount allowed as per agreement and custom	2	10	10
Brokerage for attendance at weighing and making entries at 1%	2	6	0
Commission on gross sales at 2½%	5	1	8
Total charges	105	2	1
Net proceeds	98	7	5

Source: Account and Invoice Book, Wallace, Davidson and Johnson, Maryland Hall of Records, Annapolis, Maryland.

England, and by the later colonial period the differentials were only 15 to 25 percent.

More systematic evidence on improvements in marketing and on declining distribution is available for transatlantic shipments of tobacco. Figure 9 portrays the movement of tobacco prices in Amsterdam and Philadelphia, 1720–72. The average difference between the two as a percentage of the Amsterdam price fell fairly steadily over the period:

1720–4	82%	1740–4	77%	1760–4	70%
1725–9	76%	1745–9	76%	1765–9	65%
1730–4	82%	1750–4	67%	1770–2	51%
1735–9	77%	1755–9	72%		

Productivity change in shipping

These gains were in large part due to reductions in ocean freight rates. As noted in Table 11, freight costs loomed largest among total distribution costs. Although changes in these rates varied over time and among routes, the trend

Figure 9. A comparison of Amsterdam and Philadelphia tobacco prices, 1720–72. *Source:* N. W. Posthumus, *Inquiry into the History of Prices in Holland* (Leiden: E. J. Brill, 1946), I, pp. 202–3 and 597–602, and Anne Bezanson et al., *Prices in Colonial Pennsylvania* (Philadelphia: University of Pennsylvania Press, 1935), pp. 422 and 432.

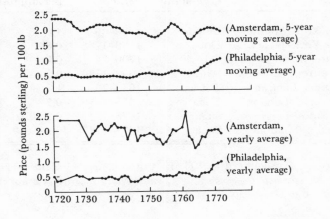

was persistently downward. Overall, they fell by approximately one-half during a century– 1675–1775.

Neither a monetary phenomenon nor a mere consequence of declines in the general price level, such a noteworthy decline in rates resulted from productivity advances in shipping that raised output relative to the inputs used. Table 12, giving approximate measures of the rates of productivity change by commodity route, shows the rate of growth of output (ton-miles freighted) relative to the rate of growth of labor and capital in combination on these routes. As we shall later see, by the standards of the day these were very high rates of productivity change. They suggest that shipping was improving faster than were other sectors and that it became a strategic factor in the overall economic advance of the period.

Inputs per voyage

To determine the source of this advance in productivity we must assess the inputs used in shipping. Two factors must be

Table 12. *Changes in shipping productivity by commodity route*

Route	Commodity	Period	Annual rates of increase per annum (%)
New York–London	Bullion	1700–89	1.0
New York–Jamaica	Flour	1699–1768	0.8
Boston–London	Oil	1700–74	0.9
So. Europe–London	Wine	1650–1770	0.6
Virginia–London	Tobacco	1630–75	1.2
Maryland–London	Tobacco	1676–1776	0.7
Barbados–London	Sugar	1678–1717	0.9
Jamaica–London	Sugar	1678–1717	0.9

Source: J. F. Shepherd and G.M. Walton, *Shipping, Maritime Trade and the Economic Development of Colonial North America* (Cambridge: Cambridge University Press, 1972), p. 69.

weighed: the labor and capital employed on a single voyage and the time component or the number of voyages taken per ship per year.

An important aspect of shipping in general has been the effect of ship size on costs per ton-mile. Where trade was well organized and the market large, *economies of scale* could be realized. Though vessels of larger size carried larger crews, the tons per man (carrying capacity per unit of labor) were significantly greater. In other words, crew size (and labor costs) increased less than proportionately to tonnage as vessels gained in size. As Figure 10 clearly indicates, the ton-man ratio of small ships (50–99 tons) was less than half that of vessels exceeding 300 tons. One would certainly expect that such obvious economies in labor would lead to the use of larger ships, on the average, over the period. On some routes, such as those into the Baltic and noticeably on the timber trade to Norway, very large vessels (with high ton-man ratios) did indeed come into service by the early seventeenth century. However, the average size of vessels employed in the Caribbean and western Atlantic showed little long-term increase prior to the Revolution, and, discounting fluctuations, ships in colonial waters showed no upward trend over time.

Figure 10. Tons per man by size of ship in 1764. Source: *Lloyd's Register of Shipping,* 1764.

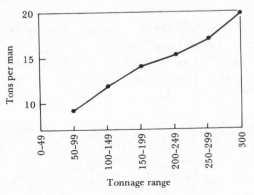

Economies of scale in shipping could not be realized in colonial waters because the nature of the numerous small and scattered markets offset any labor-saving benefits to be gained from the use of large vessels. The larger the vessel, the greater was the probability of its being underutilized, and large vessels such as a ship, snow, or brig typically faced port times as much as twice those required by schooners or by sloops. This meant that a small vessel could travel a greater average number of miles per ton than could a large vessel. Consequently, though economies of scale in shipping were available in some trade areas, these potential economies were precluded in the colonies by limited market size and by colonial commercial practices that gave rise to high risks of underutilization for large-sized ships.

Despite the lack of increase in average ship size, during the century evidence on tons per man for vessels trading in colonial waters show striking increases; evidently, then, crew sizes must have been falling for vessels of a given size. For instance, in Boston a vessel of fifty tons employed approximately seven men in 1716; by 1765 only five men were needed to crew a vessel of that size trading there. Similarly for New York, a fifty-ton vessel would employ eleven men in 1716 and only seven by 1764.

A precipitous decline in armaments also raised the efficiency of merchant vessels in the eighteenth century. Gunnery requirements varied among routes according to the likelihood of war hazards or of encounters with pirates or privateers. Originally, vessels owned in Great Britain tended to be more heavily protected than colonial vessels; however, differences in gun-man ratios diminished until they were very nearly the same in the two fleets by the Revolution. In fact, by that time guns were seldom carried on merchant vessels.

Another shipping benefit of the period was a decline in insurance rates, stemming from diminishing risks. In the seventeenth century, the customary payment in case of loss had varied between 75 and 90 percent of the total sum insured. However, just before the mid-eighteenth century a change in the insurance contract stepped up the coverage to within 1 or 2 percent of the total loss without any raise in the premium. Thus the effective cost of premiums was lowered by approximately 10 to 20 percent. Even in cases of exceptionally high risks, such as routes into Jamaican waters where rates had been well above the peacetime norm for other areas because of the high incidence of piracy, tighter policing was now yielding benefits in lowered insurance rates. In the 1720s, although most transatlantic routes had reached a common peacetime insurance rate of 2 percent (one way), the Jamaican route had been penalized by rates of 2.5 to 3 percent outgoing and 4 percent returning. By contrast, the rate from Jamaica to an English port had dropped by 1765–75 to 3 or 3.5 percent. Between New York and Jamaica, the 5 percent rate prevailing in 1720 had generally dropped to 4 percent by 1773. By the same token, on some routes from New England to such West Indian Islands as Nevis and St. Thomas, peacetime rates fell by approximately one-half between 1700 and 1770.

One other cost item – the rate of depreciation of ships – changed little over time. Although that rate varied considerably among routes traversed, the average useful life of vessels remained relatively constant throughout the period.

The time component of voyages

So far, we have considered the general inputs of a single voyage. Now it is necessary to examine how changes occurred in travel time per voyage and in the average number of voyages feasible per year.

Ship speed and time at sea are the two prime elements in this consideration. Throughout the century there was no discernible upward trend in speed, as shown in Figure 11. On the leg of the route going to the West Indies, the average speed in knots was 1.67, 1.97, 1.60, and 1.80 for the respective periods 1686–8, 1715–19, 1742–8, and 1764–5. On the return run the rates were 1.31, 2.09, 1.59, and 1.50 for the same respective years. Clearly, vessels sailing these routes were not traveling significantly faster on the eve of the Revolution than they had been nearly one hundred years earlier.

Despite the constancy of ship speed, however, round-trip voyage times did decline. Figure 12 portrays average times in port for key ports in the American and the West Indies colonies; with the single exception of Boston, these layover times fell markedly. Because a very large proportion of a sailing ship's life was spent in port, such declines contributed greatly to productivity.

Consider, for example, the Chesapeake trade. On the average, vessels engaged there were in port more than twice as long in 1694–1701 as in 1762–8. An important contributor to this change was the introduction of Scottish factors into the Chesapeake area after 1707. Scottish traders were almost certainly more efficient than their predecessors, as indicated by the thriving early growth of the tobacco trade in Scotland. Quite likely their methods of gathering the tobacco crop, and of inventorying it in barns and warehouses from which it could be quickly loaded upon arrival of their vessels, significantly shortened port times in the Chesapeake. These practices, together with their more direct route north of Ire-

Figure 11. Average speed in knots, 1686–1765: (1) New England and New York–Jamaica and Barbados; (2) Jamaica and Barbados–New England and New York. *Source:* J. F. Shepherd and G. M. Walton, *Shipping, Maritime Trade and the Economic Development of Colonial North America* (Cambridge: Cambridge University Press, 1972), p. 71.

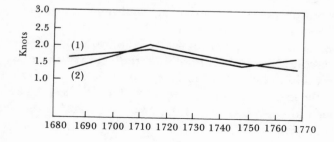

land, granted to Scottish traders a rousing bonus of two voyages per year, on average, as opposed to the single annual round trip typical of English shippers.

Similarly, in Barbados port times fell by more than half over the period. In that trade, however, quite different reasons governed the decline. In the early days, port times were extraordinarily long because the shipmasters, acting on behalf of their merchants, faced some real quandaries. Because the many scattered markets were so small and remote, prices varied widely both among islands and even for the same island over short intervals, as ships came and went. The master might have to visit several islands on a given trip to find the best market for his particular cargo. Difficulties in agreeing on prices and on the medium of exchange, plus problems of settling past debts, all slowed transactions. Often barter came into play; and even when some accepted form of exchange was used, prices were not easy to deter-

Figure 12. Average port times. *Source:* J. F. Shepherd and G. M. Walton, *Shipping, Maritime Trade and the Economic Development of Colonial North America* (Cambridge: Cambridge University Press, 1972), p. 79.

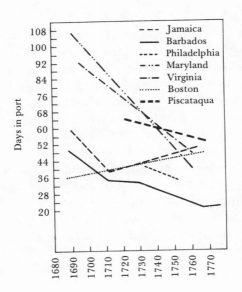

mine since the values of different currencies and bills of exchange (with varying degrees of risk) were by no means certain. In the meantime, the ship was presumably being loaded as well as unloaded, but the problem of collecting cargoes extended the stay, and when harvests were poor, port times were lengthened still further. Therefore, the real solution to long layovers in the Caribbean came with the general growth of a more systematic market economy over time.

It bears emphasis that these shortened port times for trading ships produced savings not only in capital per voyage but also in labor costs, since crews obviously had to be fed and paid while in foreign ports as well as on the voyage itself.

Such overall savings more than offset other conditions that tended during the century to raise costs per ton-mile shipped. It is true that wages and ship-repair costs remained fairly stable over the period, but costs of shipbuilding and of victualing (food for the crew) were on the rise. However, the countervailing savings led overall to gains in productivity that produced a reduction in freight costs.

Technical change, piracy and technical diffusion

Because advances in technology contributed vitally to overall improvement in the American economy during the nineteenth and twentieth centuries, we must ask what part they played in the reduction of shipping costs we have just observed. In general, it seems that technological change (defined above as an advance in knowledge) had only a minor role in this respect. Since our period preceded the era of iron ships and steam, both the materials and the power source for ship construction remained unchanged. Nor did the increasing complexity of sail and rig and the alterations of hull shapes reflect any significant advances in knowledge. Had they done so, the improvements would have shown up as an increase in ship speed over time, but no such trend is observable.

It might be argued that the reductions in crew size over time stemmed from such advances in knowledge, except that we know that during the early seventeenth century an innovative Dutch ship already displayed the essential characteristics of design, manning, and other input requirements found on the most advanced vessels in the 1760s and 1770s.

In fact, the most significant technological change that was to affect seventeenth- and eighteenth-century shipping came in approximately 1595, when the Dutch introduced the flyboat (or flute). Differing sharply from other contemporary ships, the flyboat was designed as a specialized merchant vessel for the carriage of bulk commodities. Its bottom was nearly flat, it was exceptionally long compared to its width, it was lightly built (because armament, gun platforms, and reinforced planking were eliminated), and its rig was simple. In contrast, the heavy English and colonial vessels were built, gunned, and manned to meet the dual purposes of trade and defense. Their weighty construction and armaments were costly not only in the original building but in the manning, as well. Complexity of rigging used on such vessels demanded a larger crew, as did the handling of guns in the event of attack.

The advantages of the flyboat became quickly evident when the Dutch were able to cut peacetime shipping rates by one-third to one-half. But British and colonial shippers were largely shut out from such a tempting innovation by the prevalence of pirates and privateers along the routes they frequented. In the bulk trades, where freight charges were an important fraction of final delivered prices and where the danger of attack was low, the Dutch quickly took the ascendancy, dominating the trade in the Baltic and along the English coal routes that had been cleared of pirates much earlier.

However, in the rich trades into the Mediterranean and to the East Indies, the English remained effective competitors. In fact, prohibitively high risks in all colonial waters had led to one of the most notable features of seventeenth-century shipping – the widespread use of armaments on trading vessels, still to be observed in certain waters through much of the eighteenth century. For instance, before 1750 in the Caribbean, and especially near Jamaica, vessels over 100 tons were seldom unarmed and even small vessels often carried guns.

The need for self-protection in the Caribbean is clearly described by Barbour:

> There the sea was broken by a multitude of islands affording safe anchorage and refuge, with wood, water, even provisions for the taking. There the colonies of the great European powers, grouped within a few days' sail of one another, were forever embroiled in current European wars which gave the stronger of them excuse for preying on the weaker and seemed to make legitimate the constant disorder of those seas. There trade was rich but settlement thin and defense difficult. There the idle, the criminal, and the poverty-stricken were sent to ease society in the Old World. By all these conditions piracy was fostered, and for two centuries throve ruinously, partly as an easy method of individual enrichment and partly as an instrument of practical politics.[2]

Privateering, like piracy, added to the disorder. "Letters of marque" granted by various nation-states gave private citizens license to harass the shipping of rival states.[3] Privateering commissions were issued without constraint in wartime, and even in peacetime they occasionally were given for the purpose of redress to citizens who had suffered loss from subjects of an offending state. These commissions were obtained easily: "The English and Dutch, French and Portuguese peddled letters of marque freely to one another, and regularly to the disadvantage of Spain, the rich prey in those parts."[4] Since privateers frequently ignored the constraints of their commissions in the absence of viable enforcement, privateering was hard to distinguish from common piracy.

Other official policies tended to augment these sea hazards. As though the supply of actual and potential privateers and pirates was not enough, some of the islands were deliberately peopled with convicts. As late as 1718, the governor of Jamaica complained of this policy and stated its effect in sea disorders:

> Several People have been lately sent over out of the gaols in England, upon the Encouragement of An Act of Parliament pass'd the last sessions . . . those people have been so farr from altering their Evil Courses and way of living and becoming an Advantage to Us, that the greatest part of them are gone and have Induced others to go with them a Pyrating and have Inveglied and Encouraged Severall Negroes to desert from their Masters and go to the Spaniards in Cuba, the few that remains proves a wicked Lazy and Indolent people, so that I could heartily wish this Country might be troubled with no more of them.[5]

In 1700, Colonel Query of Virginia wrote to the Council of Trade and Plantations that "all the news of America is, the swarming of pirates not only on these coasts, but all the West Indies over, which doth ruin trade ten times worse than a war."[6]

Piracy was not limited to the Caribbean. Lurking safely in the inlets of North Carolina, pirates regularly raided and looted vessels trading at Charleston, and in 1718 it was reported that "every month brought intelligence of renewed outrages, of vessels sacked on the high seas, burned with their cargo, or seized and converted to the nefarious uses of the outlaws."[7] Local traders, shippers, and government officials in the Carolinas made numerous pleas to the Board of Trade for protection, but their requests were largely ignored. In desperation, Carolina inhabitants acting through their local Assembly voted in 1719 to appropriate funds to support private vessels to rid their seas of pirates. These attempts were mostly in vain, however, and not until the Royal Navy finally took action was piracy curbed in these waters. By 1742 it was reported "the pirates on the coast have been completely extermi- nated, and vessels came and went, unarmed and un- guarded without fear of interruption."[8]

With the end of piracy, armaments could be abandoned and crew sizes reduced. Technical diffusion now became possible, and specialized cargo-carrying vessels, similar in de- sign to the flyboat, were adopted. In the process, the costs of shipping were substantially reduced, and the Atlantic trad- ing community felt the benefits.

Other improvements in distribution

A variety of other improvements not presently subject to measure probably helped in lowering distribution costs over- all. For instance, there is evidence that packaging costs de- clined as the average size of containers for important staple commodities increased substantially during the colonial pe- riod. Sugar hogsheads from the West Indies approximately doubled in weight, and barrels of rice exported from the lower South increased from an average of about 350 pounds in 1717 to about 525 pounds in the 1770s. Between 1675 and 1775, the size of tobacco hogsheads increased almost 70 percent, and tighter compression of tobacco meant that an additional 30 percent was being packaged (and shipped) per hogshead.

In itself, the enlargement of the hogsheads led to input saving per volume packaged. Although the greater size de- manded somewhat larger inputs of labor time as well as larger staves, hoops, and headings, the increased size al- lowed a more-than-proportionate increase in packaged weight. This is true because the capacity of a container such as a barrel expands more than the surface area with each increment in size. Thus it was to the shipper's advantage to increase the size of his container to the point where difficul- ties of handling would offset the economies to be gained from its use.

A lowering of inventory costs also improved the marketing of colonial commodities during this period. In the early eighteenth century, when vessels typically were held up in port for long periods, a good part of the delay had often been due to a time-consuming search for cargo. Purchases and deliveries were generally made in small lots, requiring many transactions before a vessel's holds were filled. In the Chesapeake area, for example, ships plying from farm site to farm site to gather tobacco spent nearly a hundred days in port, on the average, near the turn of the century. By 1770, those port times had been reduced to less than fifty days. In that case, most of the credit went to the innovation of specialized facilities for the storing and inventorying of tobacco, so that arriving ships now found cargoes neatly assembled and awaiting them in convenient dockside warehouses.

These observed reductions in port times also point to another likely assumption: that total inventory time was lessening for colonial planters. The span of time extending from harvest to outbound-shipping date represented the period when a grower's capital was tied up on warehouse shelves. Obviously, it was to the planter's advantage to move his crop as promptly as possible, since the alternative costs of his capital varied directly with the period for which inventories were held. In the Chesapeake area, total inventory times were reduced by at least fifty days, and similar reductions were noted elsewhere.

Another, and perhaps the most important, improvement to affect the costs of distribution during the eighteenth century was the decline of risks associated with trade. As we have already seen earlier, a barometer of this improvement was the lowering of insurance rates on overseas shipments. Despite a wide variation between war and peacetime, or such factors as seasonal threats of hurricanes in the Caribbean, average insurance rates declined notably between 1675 and 1775.[9]

We have already noted the reasons for the lowering of insurance rates. Pirates and privateers had been suppressed, trade and commerce were becoming established ways of life, and the probability was steadily increasing that any given cargo would come safely into port.

The cost of credit was another factor that had to be taken into account in trade between the Old World and the New. The normal procedure was for the English merchant to include a twelve-month interest charge in the price of goods shipped to the colonies, the charge to be reimbursed in full or in part if payment were completed before the end of that period. The fact that this system was in general use suggests that short-term credit was an accepted fact of life in transatlantic trade. Therefore the general reduction in interest rates throughout the eighteenth century served further to lower prices on colonial imports.

In summary, then, the observed reductions in distribution costs throughout the century were caused by essentially the same forces that were lowering shipping costs. Technological change played no significant role, but economies of scale acted more effectively than in shipping. The decline of piracy and privateering reduced insurance rates on cargoes as well as on vessels. Productivity advances in packaging resulted from *learning by doing*. For instance, with tobacco, it took time and experience to discover what size of hogshead would minimize packaging costs although still permitting easy handling. Economies of scale probably lowered inventory costs. The growing scale of production also allowed for the development of specialized storage facilities whose costs of organization demanded some minimum level of transactions. In turn, these facilities were largely responsible for reductions in ship layovers. Finally, the burgeoning of trade and the development of European credit institutions caused interest rates to drop. One further effect of the increased trade was to lower risks and thus to reinforce commercial expansion.

Productivity change in colonial agriculture

Although productivity changes in shipping and distribution were rapid by the standards of the day, it must be remembered that commerce remained a relatively small part of the overall economy. The dominant sector was agriculture. Therefore, improvements in productivity and efficiency for the entire economy depended heavily on the progress of agriculture.

Recent investigations focused on nineteenth-century agriculture have uncovered some clues to the rates of advance during colonial times. For the nineteenth century as a whole, productivity in agriculture improved at an annual average rate approximating 0.5 percent.[10] However, the rate accelerated over the century: the first half had produced a rate only between 0.1 and 0.2 percent as compared to a latter-half advance of 0.8 percent. Clearly it is reasonable to expect that the eighteenth-century experience would mirror more closely the immediately following period. We would assume, therefore, that productivity in agriculture improved at a relatively slow rate during colonial times.

Historical descriptions reinforce that conclusion. For instance, for the colonies north of the Chesapeake area we are told that "the eighteenth century farmers showed little advance over the first settlers in their care of livestock"; and "little if any improvements had been made in farm implements until the very close of the eighteenth century."[11] Another study, on Pennsylvania agriculture, concludes that "economic conditions throughout the century prohibited major changes and encouraged a reasonably stable and uniform type of mixed farming that involved fairly extensive use or superficial working of the land."[12]

A more recent investigation of productivity change in Pennsylvania agriculture measures these qualitative assertions in quantitative terms.[13] The new findings bear out that rates of productivity change were indeed low for the eighteenth century; nevertheless it appears that modest progress was made and that output did rise relative to the inputs of the available land, capital, and labor.

Evidence on levels of output and use of factors of production per farm in Pennsylvania (given in Table 13) shows that

Pennsylvania farming was becoming more capital-intensive and less labor-intensive over the century. Capital inputs increased relative to labor and to land, and both capital and land increased relative to labor per average farm.

Cleared land per farm changed little during the period, and the size of the average farm declined sharply, from approximately 500 acres near 1700 to about 130 or 140 acres in the late colonial period. Most of this, however, was due to the subdivision of uncleared acres and the creation of new farms, with little change in the average of cleared acres per farm. Uncleared land is almost entirely irrelevant in measuring land input for the place and time we are considering, since uncleared acres per farm far exceeded any minimum needs for fuel and timber, so that variations in uncleared land had no noticeable effect on output. Capital inputs per farm increased, however, as more implements,

Table 13. *Indexes of inputs, outputs, and productivity in Pennsylvania agriculture, 1700–1800*

Years	(1) Land	(2) Capital	(3) Labor	(4) Combined inputs[a]	(5) Livestock	(6) Grain	(7) Total output[b]	(8) (7)/(4) Output Input
1714–31	100	100	100	100	100	100	100	100
1734–45	100	114	91	95	103	100	101	106
1750–70	106	126	91	97	106	103	107	110
1775–90	106	121	88	97	87	110	103	109

Notes: [a]The combined inputs index is obtained by weighting land, capital, and labor at 14, 10, and 76, respectively.

[b]Total output is adjusted to include some nonagriculture output after 1750, therefore influencing the total output index slightly in the last two periods.

Source: Duane Ball and Gary M. Walton, "Agricultural Productivity Change in Eighteenth Century Pennsylvania," *Journal of Economic History,* XXVI (1976), Tables 4, 5, and 7.

structures, and inventories accumulated. A decrease in labor per farm was due largely to the large but decreasing size of families during the century.

In combination, total input declined slightly per farm. Nevertheless, output per farm was growing. Not only was the average Pennsylvania farm producing more livestock and grains (mainly wheat and "meslyn," a combination of wheat and rye), but by late colonial times we observe a limited increase in nonagricultural output as some farm labor took on such part-time occupations as milling, smithing, tanning, cabinetmaking, and chairmaking. Altogether, the average output per farm increased by about 7 percent (1713–31 to 1750–70).

The productivity advance (that is, the rise of output relative to the combined input) was nearly 10 percent over the eighteenth century, implying an annual rate of change of approximately 0.2 percent. Rising most rapidly in the early period (0.3 to 0.4 percent), the rate of increase had slowed by mid-century. During the decades just following the American Revolution, productivity quite understandably appears to have declined slightly in the aftermath of war and in the face of market adjustments to the new-found independence. In any case, productivity in Pennsylvania agriculture did begin in the colonial period a rise that continued at a rate between 0.2 and 0.3 percent up until the Revolution. Though less vigorous than rates of advance in shipping, such improvement strengthened the agricultural base and helped stimulate urbanization and economic progress in other sectors as well.

The causes of productivity advance in Pennsylvania agriculture appear primarily to have stemmed from farmers learning how to use the soil and their implements more effectively. There are no signs of economies of scale, as would be indicated by enlargement of farms or by technological improvements. However, better business organization and greater market participation may have contributed to the gains in productivity.

Although the information on earlier periods is limited, there is reason to believe that the seventeenth century may have witnessed greater gains in productivity than did the eighteenth. For instance, Table 12 shows that productivity change in shipping was higher in the 1630–75 period than thereafter. Additional evidence on tobacco, the major colonial export, suggests significant productivity advances in the early seventeenth century, with little further increases thereafter. As shown in Figure 13, the price per pound of tobacco in the Chesapeake area fell sharply soon after its introduction there. The first and most rapid phase of this price decline ended near 1630, only a dozen years after the begin-

Figure 13. Price of Chesapeake tobacco, 1618–1714. *Sources:* 1618–58, 1711–14 – Russell R. Menard, "The Chesapeake Economy, 1618–1720: An Interpretation" (unpublished paper presented at the Johns Hopkins University Seminar on the Atlantic Community, November 20, 1973), Figure 1: 1659–1710 – Russell R. Menard, "Farm Prices of Maryland Tobacco, 1659–1710," *Maryland Historical Magazine,* LVIII (Spring 1973), p. 85.

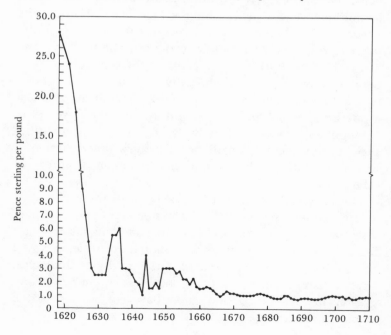

ning of tobacco cultivation in the Chesapeake area. A second phase developed over the following three decades, followed by a long period of low and relatively stable prices. There can be little doubt that these two phases of declining tobacco prices represented surges in productivity that produced lower costs per unit. Since production increased greatly, as shown in Figure 14, the decline in price obviously was not due to lowered demand in Europe or elsewhere. Rather, costs per pound fell in unison with rising output relative to inputs. The limited evidence on prices of inputs, mainly for labor and land, suggests no decline and perhaps a modest increase over those years. Table 14, giving prices for indentured servants, perhaps indicates a slight rise in such labor costs. Similarly, average prices for adult slaves in Virginia rose from a little under to a little over £20 during these years. Land prices also rose slightly. Therefore no reduction of input prices could claim credit for the observed lowering

Figure 14. Quantity of American tobacco imported into Great Britain, 1618–1714 (thousands of pounds). *Sources:* 1639–Lewis Cecil Gray, *History of Agriculture in the Southern United States to 1860* (Washington, D.C.: 1933), I, p. 213; all other years–Russell R. Menard, "The Chesapeake Economy," Figure 1.

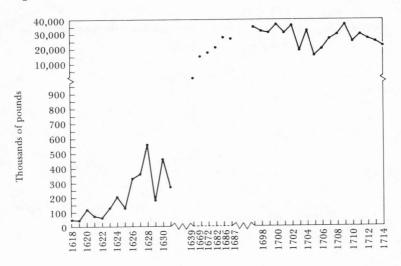

of costs. This must have stemmed from productivity advances, which, in terms of annual rates of change, were undoubtedly higher in the early colonial period than in the eighteenth century.

A fair share of all advances in the colonial period must be attributed to trial-and-error experimentation. "Learning by doing" was the order of the day, whereby seeds, soil, implements, labor, and all the other inputs of an agricultural economy gradually found their optimum uses. And it seems that much of this wisdom was accumulated in the seventeenth century.

In fact, the greatest gains of all perhaps were achieved in the period between the earliest starvation-subsistence phase and the adoption of commercial agricultural practices near the middle of the seventeenth century.

Despite the slowing, it is evident that progress took place, if only haltingly, during the entire colonial period. Wars and other disruptions only temporarily impeded its determined advance.

Table 14. *Price of male indentured servants with terms of four years or more, 1662–1709*

Year	Price (£)	Year	Price (£)
1662–4	10	1686–8	11/10s.
1665–7	9	1689–1	12
1668–70	10	1692–4	10
1671–3	8/10s.	1695–7	10/10s.
1674–6	8	1698–1700	11/10s.
1677–80	9	1701–3	12
1680–2	11	1704–6	12/10s.
1683–5	10/10s.	1707–9	11

Source: Russell R. Menard, Economy and Society in Early Colonial Maryland (Ph.D. dissertation, University of Iowa, 1975), Table VII-2, p. 342.

Glossary of terms

Technological change
  Technological change is an advance in knowledge that permits more output to be produced from the same amount of inputs (resources).

Technical diffusion
  Technical diffusion is the spread of known techniques of production from one producing unit to another.

Investment in human capital
  Investment in human capital refers to such things as training, education, and medical and nutritional attention given people that improves the quality of labor, and therefore increases their contribution to production and yields higher incomes in the future. Investment may be formal, such as schooling, or informal, such as on-the-job training.

Economies of scale
  Economies of scale exist when the average cost of producing a particular good or service decreases as the quantity of this good or service produced increases.

Learning by doing
  Learning by doing refers to the improvements in productivity that typically occur over time with a new production process. The improvements stem from experience and increasing familiarity with the techniques employed in the new process.

Selected readings

Ball, Duane E., and Gary M. Walton, "Agricultural Productivity Change in Eighteenth-Century Pennsylvania," *Journal of Economic History*, XXXVI, 1 (March 1976), pp. 102–17.

Shepherd, James F., and Gary M. Walton, *Shipping, Maritime Trade, and the Economic Development of Colonial North America* (Cambridge: Cambridge University Press, 1972), Chapters 4, 5.

Shepherd, James F., and Gary M. Walton, "Trade, Distribution, and Economic Growth in Colonial America," *Journal of Economic History*, XXXII, 1 (March 1972), pp. 128–45.

7

Growth and distribution of colonial income and wealth

The rate of growth of income

There can be little doubt that total output expanded rapidly over the colonial period. Both the rapid rate of population growth, and the rising volume of exports and imports and tonnage of vessels entering and clearing colonial ports, suggest a rapid acceleration of aggregate output. Unfortunately, we lack any accurate measures of the growth of real per-capita output by which to assess the long-run trend rate of growth in the colonies. The best that can be done is to make some educated guesses about probable rates of economic growth based upon qualitative and less-then-complete quantitative evidence which has survived.

The evidence presented in the preceding chapter clearly implies that output per capita did increase over the colonial period. Greater productivity in shipping and distribution lowered the real costs of these services, and, as we saw earlier, this stimulus from trade resulted in patterns of regional specialization and in greater market participation, both of which served to increase output per capita. In addition, the evidence pertaining to colonial Pennsylvania agriculture suggests that here, too, output was advancing relative to total input over the eighteenth century. Workers on Chester County farms, for example, increased their output during that time by approximately 0.3 to 0.4 percent per year, with the fastest rate for this growth occurring during the early decades.

In addition, the evidence suggests that the most rapid rates of productivity advance came early, during the period of first settlement. This was revealed in shipping, in Pennsylvania agriculture, and also in the evidence on tobacco prices. Generally then, the rise in productivity occurred early on (in the seventeenth century, in the case of tobacco production), and subsequent advances were modest by comparison. As we shall see later in this chapter, the same early-rise pattern also applies to colonial wealth per capita.

Following the hazardous initial period of settlement and experimentation with agriculture, the colonists quickly established a comfortable subsistence base. Soon a moderate surplus was being realized for sale, first in local markets and then (most crucially for the economy) for export. Inevitably, the growth of income and wealth kept step.

Such progress was largely attributable to economies stemming from increased specialization. And this, in turn, resulted from a learning process: the colonists had not only learned what to produce and how to produce it most efficiently; they also had learned the techniques of preparing land, structures, and tools and equipment (the necessary physical capital) for that efficient production. Once these had been realized, the basis for growth diminished and growth rates declined and remained at lower rates.

In summary, then, we conclude that living standards, though varying from area to area depending on the timing of initial settlement, did increase on average, more rapidly in the seventeenth century than in the eighteenth century. There is general agreement that improvements in living standards in the colonies occurred throughout the colonial period. As Bruchey states:

At the outset of the colonial experience the settlers in Virginia went through a "starving period": by January of the second year of Jamestown's settlement, 67 of the original 105 colonists were dead of disease and malnutrition. But in 1663 the Reverend John Higginson of

Boston could observe that "we live in a more plentifull
and comfortable manner than ever we did expect." And
by the 1740's Benjamin Franklin could remark that
"The first drudgery of settling new colonies, which con-
fines the attention of people to mere necessaries, is now
pretty well over; and there are many in every province
in circumstances that set them at ease . . . "[1]

Alternatively, there is strong support for the presumption
that the economy grew at a faster rate in the nineteenth
century than in the colonial period. Raymond W. Goldsmith
has pointed out that if the trend rate of growth of 1.6 percent for the period 1839–1960 is extrapolated back into the
period before 1839, unrealistic figures are soon reached.

If the trend observed since 1839 had been in force before that date, average income per head in today's
[1959] prices would have been about $145 in 1776, $80
in 1739, and less than $30 in 1676. It takes only a little
consideration of the minimum requirements for keeping body and soul together, even in the simpler conditions prevailing in colonial America, to conclude that at
present prices for individual commodities an average
level of income below $200 is fairly well ruled out for
1776 or even the early eighteenth century.[2]

Many scholars like Goldsmith have thought that the long-
term rate of growth in the United States accelerated sometime prior to 1840 and that consequently its history was
marked by discontinuity. In questioning whether there was a
single upturn in the American rate of economic growth
prior to 1840 (the year systematic estimates of a gross national product begin), Paul David has recently suggested
perhaps there was more than one period of acceleration.[3]
Others have speculated on a specific growth rate for the
colonial period. Using statistical fragments and qualitative
evidence, George Rogers Taylor has suggested that the
growth of real product per capita before 1710 was slow and

irregular, and that between 1710 and 1775 it averaged "slightly more than one percent per annum."[4] Taylor's suggested rate of growth is higher than others, however, and his estimatè may embody a confusion between levels and rates of change. Undoubtedly living standards were higher in the eighteenth century than in the seventeenth, but according to our contention, rates of growth of income were higher in the seventeenth. In view of the predominance of agriculture, and the low rates of apparent productivity improvement in that sector in the eighteenth century, it is difficult to imagine that the growth of output per capita could have equaled even 1 percent per year.

Recently, Robert Gallman has concurred in the belief that the average annual rate of growth in eighteenth-century colonial America was considerably below 1 percent.[5] From evidence based upon factor supplies, he places it between 0.3 and 0.5 percent for the period 1710–1840. From the evidence on productivity change both in agriculture and in shipping and distribution, we speculate that the rate of growth for the eighteenth century must have been lower than modern rates, slightly below 0.5 percent per annum. It might be noted the trend rate of growth of output per head estimated for England during the eighteenth century up to 1785 is 0.3 percent per year.[6]

Growth rates in the colonies were probably roughly similar to those in England. They did, however, vary sharply among regions, especially in the newly settled areas where, as we have seen, a spurt of growth followed the learning by experimenting process. Thus we would expect that in the earlier part of the eighteenth century the younger settlements of the middle colonies and the lower South would enjoy a faster rate of growth than would the Chesapeake and New England areas, where the growth rate had undoubtedly been higher in the seventeenth century. In a recent study of wealth accumulation in New England between 1650 and 1710, Terry Anderson has concluded that real wealth per person increased in that region at an annual rate of 1.6 percent.[7] Although the advance of income per capita may not have paralleled this rise of wealth per person, his findings do suggest that rates of growth of output may have been higher in the seventeenth century in New England than were to be sustained throughout the entire colonial period.

Levels of income in the late colonial period

Whatever the rate of colonial growth, the levels of income per free colonist on the eve of the American Revolution were certainly extraordinarily high. The evidence for this is found principally in recent studies based upon colonial probate records by Alice Hanson Jones,[8] Jackson Turner Main,[9] and others. Jones's estimates derived from such records suggest that in 1774 the average free person held wealth in the value of £76 (see Table 15). In terms of purchasing power,

Table 15. *Private physical wealth per free person, 1774 (£)*

	New England	Middle colonies	Southern colonies	Total 13 colonies
Land	27	28	55	38
Servants and slaves	0	2	58	21
Livestock	3	5	9	6
Farm tools and household equipment	1	1	3	2
Crops and perishables	1	3	5	3
Consumer durables	4	4	6	5
Other	2	3	1	2
Total	38	46	137	76

Note: All figures have been rounded to the nearest pound sterling. Components may not add to total due to rounding.
Source: Alice Hanson Jones, "Components of Private Wealth per Free Capita for the 13 Colonies by Region, 1774," in U.S. Bureau of Census, *Historical Statistics: Colonial Times to 1970* (Washington, D.C.: Government Printing Office, 1976), Series Z, 169–212, p. 1175.

the pound then equaled just under $38 in 1973 prices; thus the average free colonist was worth approximately $2,860 in modern holdings (thereby excluding slaves and indentured servants).

Such high levels of wealth deserve considerable emphasis. As a general rule, wealth-stock estimates can be converted into income flows by dividing the wealth estimates by *capital-output ratios*. The relationship between capital and output (the capital-output ratio) depends upon a host of influences and varies both over time and among countries and regions. Nevertheless, under normal peacetime conditions, the ratio is seldom lower than three nor higher than five. If such ratios held true in the late colonial period, then we may estimate a possible range of colonial income per free person. By this process Jones's findings suggest that annual per-capita income of free colonists stood in the range of £15 to £25 (in 1774 prices), or $573 to $955 in 1973 prices.[10]

In general, the estimates point to surprisingly high standards of living for the world of that time. As revealed in Table 16, relatively few countries today enjoy average income levels achieved in the American colonies on the eve of independence. In fact, more than two-thirds of the world population today lives in countries where average income is below that of the average free American two hundred years ago. This is true for most of the Third World, including China, India, and large parts of Africa and South America. Colonial Americans, free of bondage, lived relatively well.

The distribution of wealth, 1774

Although the figure of £76 indicates substantial well-being for the average free American in the late colonial period, we must emphasize that the bounty was far from equally distributed. As shown in Table 15, physical wealth per free person varied sharply among the regions. By far the richest was the South, where average wealth holdings per free person were more than double those in New England and in the middle

Table 16. *Population and GNP per capita by income group, 1973*

Income groups	Number of countries	Population (millions)	Average GNP per capita (US$)
Less than $200	43	1,151	120
$200–$499	52	1,184	280
$500–$1,999	53	531	1,000
$2,000–$4,999	28	654	2,860
Over $5,000	12	316	5,970

Countries with per-capita income less than $200

Afghanistan
Bangladesh
Benin (People's Rep. of)
Bhutan
Burma
Burundi
Cambodia
Central African Rep.
Chad
Comoro Islands
Ethiopia
Gambia
Guinea
Haiti
India
Indonesia
Kenya
Laos
Lesotho
Malagasy Rep.
Malawi
Maldive Islands
Mali
Nepal
Niger
Pakistan
Portuguese Timor
Rwanda
Sierra Leone
Sikkim
Somalia
South Vietnam
Sri Lanka
Sudan
Tanzania
Togo
Uganda
Upper Volta
Vietnam (Dem. Rep. of)
Yemen Arab Rep.
Yemen (People's Dem. Rep. of)
Zaire

Countries with per capita income $200–$499

Albania
Angola
Antigua
Bolivia
Botswana
British Solomon Islands
Cameroon
Cape Verde Islands
China (People's Rep. of)
Colombia
Congo (People's Rep. of)
Dominica
Ecuador
Egypt (Arab Rep. of)
El Salvador
Equatorial Guinea
Ghana
Gilbert and Ellice Islands
Grenada
Guinea–Bissau
Guyana
Honduras
Ivory Coast
Jordan
Korea (Dem. Rep. of)
Korea (Rep. of)
Liberia
Macao
Mauritania
Mauritius
Morocco
Mozambique
New Hebrides
Nigeria
Papua New Guinea
Paraguay
Philippines
Rhodesia
São Tomé & Principe
Senegal
Seychelles Islands
St. Kitts–Nevis–Anguilla
St. Lucia
St. Vincent
Swaziland
Syrian Arab Rep.
Thailand
Tonga
Trust Terr. of the Pacific Is.
Western Samoa
Zambia

Countries with per capita income of $500–$1,999

Algeria	Fr. Terr. of Afars and Issas	Netherlands Antilles
American Samoa	Gabon	Nicaragua
Argentina	Gibraltar	Oman
Bahrain	Greece	Panama
Barbados	Guadeloupe	Peru
Belize	Guatemala	Portugal
Brazil	Hong Kong	Reunion
Brunei	Hungary	Romania
Bulgaria	Iran	Saudi Arabia
Ceuta & Melilla	Iraq	Singapore
Chile	Isle of Man	South Africa
China (Rep. of)	Jamaica	Spain
Costa Rica	Lebanon	Surinam
Cuba	Malaysia	Trinidad and Tobago
Cyprus	Malta	Turkey
Dominican Rep.	Martinique	Uruguay
Fiji	Mexico	Venezuela
French Guiana	Mongolia	Yugoslavia

Countries with per-capita income $2,000–$4,999

Australia	France	Libyan Arab Rep.
Austria	French Polynesia	Luxembourg
Bahamas	German Dem. Rep.	Netherlands
Belgium	Greenland	New Zealand
Bermuda	Guam	Norway
Canal Zone	Ireland	Poland
Channel Islands	Israel	Puerto Rico
Czechoslovakia	Italy	United Kingdom
Faeroe Islands	Japan	USSR
Finland		

Countries with per-capita income of $5,000–over

Canada	Kuwait	United States
Denmark	New Caledonia	Sweden
Germany (Fed. Rep. of)	Qatar	Switzerland
Iceland	United Arab Emirates	Virgin Islands (U.S.)

Source: World Bank Atlas: Population, Per Capita Product and Growth Rates (Washington, D.C.: International Bank for Reconstruction and Development, 1975) p. 8.

colonies. That this striking differential between regions was not due simply to divergence in the holdings of servants and slaves is clear from the table. Although that classification shows the most striking contrast, differences between the regions are also of the order of two to one per free person in the categories of livestock, producer durables, farm tools and household equipment, and inventories. Even the value of land holdings per free person in the South was more than twice those in New England or the middle colonies.

Evidence from the probate records also indicates the distribution of wealth was highly unequal among individuals within regions. Based on the recent work of a number of historians, the figures show that wealth was far from evenly divided among the population by the end of the colonial period. (Until these new studies, it had been widely accepted that wealth, and presumably income, had been quite equitably distributed until the early nineteenth century brought the onset of industrialization.)

The situation in the middle colonies and New England is pictured in Table 17. These estimates by Alice Hanson Jones are based on 1774 probate records from counties selected by random sampling procedures; thus they are designed to represent typical wealth holdings for the entire region in each case. An obvious bias is introduced by the fact that probate data relate only to those who have died, hence they are more representative of those in the older age bracket, who would be assumed to have accumulated more wealth. To estimate wealth owned by the living, then, an adjustment had to be made relating the (known) age of the decedents to the age composition of the living population.

The estimates in Table 17 have been adjusted for this factor; thus they may be taken to show the distribution of wealth for that part of the living population whose estates were likely to be probated. And these estimates do indeed show a widespread inequality. In New England the wealthiest 10 percent of this portion of the population owned 40 percent of the wealth, and in the middle colonies 32 percent.

The poorer half of this group owned only 11 percent and 23 percent of the wealth in New England and in the middle colonies, respectively, leaving 89 percent and 77 percent in these regions for the wealthy half.

What can be known about the distribution of wealth for the entire population? Since not all decedents were probated, nothing can be said with certainty. It is known that some decedents whose estates were not probated did have some (even considerable) wealth. Many others, however, probably left little or no estate, and one suspects that the bias would be in this latter direction. If this presumption is correct, the estimates in Table 17 would understate the degree of inequality in these two regions.

Professor Jones has also recently examined the distribution of wealth for the southern colonies.[11] Even when excluding slaves as a form of wealth (an omission which would

Table 17. *Distribution of physical wealth in New England, 1770, and the middle colonies, 1774*

Cumulative proportion of wealth held by	New England	Middle colonies
Poorest 10%	less than 1	less than 1
Poorest 20%	1	2
Poorest 50%	11	23
Richest 20%	60	47
Richest 10%	40	32

Note: These estimates of wealth are based upon probated decedents, adjusted to the age composition of the living population for selected counties in New England and the middle colonies. They include land, slaves, and portable physical wealth (producers' and consumers' durables), but exclude cash and financial assets.
Source: Alice Hanson Jones, "Wealth Estimates for the New England Colonies about 1770," *Journal of Economic History*, XXXII (1972), p. 119, and "Wealth Estimates for the American Middle Colonies, 1774," *Economic Development and Cultural Change*, XVIII (1970), part 2.

of course have greater effect in the southern colonies than in the northern), her estimates for this region show a still greater disparity in the distribution of wealth than she discovered for the middle colonies and New England.

Trends in the distribution of income and wealth

This picture of unbalanced wealth holdings at the end of the colonial period raises several questions. One concerns the longer-term trends in the distribution. Did the inequality of the 1770s increase over time from earlier years in the colonial period? When did this concentration begin, and what were the longer-term trends in later years? If concentration of income and wealth did increase over time, what were the reasons?

According to Jackson Turner Main and others, growing concentration did occur over the colonial period. From his work in the probate records for the years around the time of the American Revolution, Main has classified four types of settlements: frontier, subsistence farming, commercial farming, and urban.[12] As settlement and economic development proceeded, a given area would progress from one stage to another, with subsistence farming giving way to greater and livelier activity (production for the market). In Main's opinion, this increasing commercialization resulted in greater inequality in wealth and, as a corollary, in a wider spread in the distribution of income as well.

Similarly, studies by James Henretta[13] and, more recently, by Bruce C. Daniels[14] both suggest a growing inequality of wealth distribution over time. Henretta analyzed two Boston tax lists of 1687 and 1771, finding that in 1687 the top 10 percent of Boston's taxpayers owned 42 percent of its wealth, whereas in 1771 they owned 57 percent. However, these conclusions are based upon only two tax lists and apply only to Boston. Daniels, using data systematically sampled from New England probate records, was able to provide more information on eighteenth-century trends in wealth concentration for this region. The study tentatively confirms Main's contention that when economic activity grows more complex it tends to produce a greater concentration of wealth. That is to say, when subsistence production for one's own family gives way to production for market, the interdependence among producers seems to be accompanied by greater disparity in wealth. Daniels found this trend both in older and in more recently settled agricultural areas, such as Suffolk and Worcester counties, in Massachusetts, and in small to medium-sized Connecticut towns. The exceptions were two larger urban places, Boston and Hartford (Connecticut), both of which seemed to exhibit a stable distribution of wealth through the eighteenth century to 1776, probably because they had been well established by 1700. One would expect that the typical increase in concentration had already taken place in these towns during the earlier period, and evidence from Portsmouth, New Hampshire, supports this view. Unlike Boston and Hartford, Portsmouth was a small village whose growth came principally after 1700, and there Daniels finds the percentage of wealth owned by the top 30 percent of the populace rising from about 65 percent in 1700–20 to 79 percent in 1760–76. The data suggest, then, not only an increasing concentration of wealth over time but that this concentration was greater in the towns than in the countryside.

Do these trends continue after the American Revolution? Further research indicates that they do. Main[15] estimates that in 1780 the wealthiest 10 percent of families owned 50 percent of the wealth, and Robert Gallman's estimate for the same decile of the population for 1860 was 70 percent. Consequently, we can say that even the early development of the American economy produced an increasing concentration of wealth that clearly preceded widespread industrialization or the formation of an urban labor force in the ninetenth century.[16]

Such a trend accompanying American development seems to be part and parcel of the process of commercialization, as production for market sale increased its share of total output. In agriculture this may have resulted from the growing pressure of population on land. As the rural population expanded, land ownership and the return from land (rent) appear to have become more concentrated. The planter class in the South is the most obvious example, though similar concentration also took place in northern agriculture. The growing use of indentured and slave labor beginning in the late seventeenth century furthered the inequality.

In towns and cities a merchant class was meantime gaining ground. Especially in the port towns, those merchant-ship-owners engaging in the export-import trade were usually found among the upper elements of society. On the other side of the scale, urbanization and industrialization were giving rise to a relatively new group: a free labor force owning no property. Thus in this early period, occupation and land ownership were major factors in the widening gap between various social groups in the colonies. As evidenced in the probate records, sex also was a factor. As a class, women owned far less property than men, and their opportunities to gain wealth were restricted.

Conclusion

This review of the evidence on colonial wealth and income has reached several tentative conclusions. By 1776, Americans clearly had achieved relatively high standards of living. The probate records show that the colonists over time had gradually acquired material possessions and luxuries. The wealth estimates tentatively show that the average free colonist fared better than his or her typical British counterpart by the end of the colonial period and probably even as early as the latter part of the seventeenth century. At the very least, we can say with assurance that material progress and economic growth did occur.

But what about the rate of this progress? If long-term wealth–output ratios held relatively constant during the colonial period, then estimates of wealth would indicate a slower overall rate of growth than the United States has experienced since 1840, the year when output data become available. However, if we can rely on those wealth estimates that indicate tentatively that higher rates of growth occurred during the earlier period of development in the seventeenth century, then we may assume that the ratio was not constant but subject to ups and downs. There is general agreement, in fact, that the rate of growth took some upturn earlier than 1840 and probably later than 1790. We suggest, then, that a similarly faster pace did indeed mark the rate of growth in the seventeenth century, followed by slower growth over the eighteenth century and lasting until an upturn sometime after 1790.

Finally, we have seen that the distribution of wealth, and almost certainly of income, became less and less evenhanded throughout the colonial period, a finding at variance with the commonly accepted view that preindustrial America was an egalitarian society. The same trend seems to have accompanied economic development well into the nineteenth century.

Glossary of terms

Gross national product (GNP)
The gross national product is the market value of all final goods and services produced in a nation during a period. When GNP is corrected for changes in the general level of prices, it is called *real* GNP (or GNP in constant prices).

Capital-output ratio
The capital-output ratio is the ratio of the total value of the existing stock of capital to the total value of output (GNP). Its importance is that it indicates how much capital is needed as an input in order to produce a certain amount of output. Equivalently, if one knows the value of the capital stock, the value of output (or income) may be inferred.

The economic rise of early America

Selected readings

Anderson, Terry L., "Wealth Estimates for the New England Colonies, 1650–1709," *Explorations in Economic History,* XII, 2 (April 1975), pp. 151–76.

Anderson, Terry L., and Robert P. Thomas, "The Rate of Growth in the Seventeenth Century Chesapeake Colonies," *Explorations in Economic History,* XV, 4 (October 1978).

David, Paul, "The Growth of Real Product in the United States before 1840: New Evidence, Controlled Conjectures," *Journal of Economic History,* XXVII, 2 (June 1967), pp. 151–97.

Gallman, Robert E., "The Pace and Pattern of American Economic Growth," in Lance E. Davis *et al., American Economic Growth: An Economist's History of the United States.* (New York: Harper & Row, 1972), pp. 15–60.

Henretta, James, "Economic Development and Social Structure in Colonial Boston," *William and Mary Quarterly,* XXII, 1 (January 1965), pp. 93–105.

Jones, Alice Hanson, "Wealth Estimates for the American Middle Colonies, 1774," *Economic Development and Cultural Change,* XVIII, 2 (July 1970), supplement, pp. 1–172.

"Wealth Estimates for the New England Colonies about 1770," *Journal of Economic History,* XXXII, 1 (March 1972), pp. 98–127.

Klingaman, David, "Food Surpluses and Deficits in the American Colonies, 1768–1772," *Journal of Economic History,* XXXI, 3 (September 1971), pp. 553–69.

Main, Gloria L., "Inequality in Early America: The Evidence of Probate Records from Massachusetts and Maryland," *Journal of Interdisciplinary History,* VII (1977), pp. 559–81.

Main, Jackson Turner, *The Social Structure of Revolutionary America* (Princeton, N.J.: Princeton University Press, 1965).

"Trends in Wealth Concentration before 1860," *Journal of Economic History,* XXXI, 2 (June 1971), pp. 445–7.

Taylor, George Rogers, "American Economic Growth before 1840: An Exploratory Essay," *Journal of Economic History,* XXIV, 4 (December 1964), pp. 427–44.

8

British bungling and the call to arms

The dozen years from the end of the Seven Years' War to the shots at Lexington saw great political friction between the colonies and the mother country. It must not be forgotten that before 1763 the colonies and Great Britain had enjoyed a century and half of harmony and reasonable goodwill. Suddenly and with acceleration, that amiable relationship deteriorated. As we know, the chain of events was ultimately linked to armed conflict.

The sparks of revolt were clearly visible during those years and as we shall see they clearly illuminate the points of friction between the mother country and her American colonies. But it is impossible to grasp the forces of revolt from those dozen years alone. It is only in the context of the longer period that we can understand the unique set of circumstances that unfolded between 1763 and 1775 that precipitated the clash of two determined peoples. *For what caused the Americans to revolt was not so much a desire to achieve independence as it was a determination to hold onto an already established freedom that was being threatened.*

Freedom for the taking

As citizens of the empire, colonists in British North America were nominally subject to much the same set of laws and restrictions, and held similar allegiances as all other Britons. Actually, however, until 1763 the only viable restrictions on colonial freedom were in matters of trade – its direction and

153

organization, both between the colonies and other parts of the empire, and between the colonies and alien countries. In all other matters, the mainland colonists enjoyed local autonomy and practical freedom in dealing with their own affairs.

Colonial governments, patterned after that of the mother country, were composed of executive and legislative branches. In each colony the legislature served as "representatives of the people." The governor, on the other hand, was expected to represent the will of the Crown, to encourage laws that added to its cohesion and strength, and to veto legislation deemed contrary to its interests.

As one might expect in an age before democracy, governors were generally appointed, either by the colony's proprietor or by the king for the royal colonies. Connecticut and Rhode Island were exceptions to the rule; there, the governor was chosen in general elections and obviously would have felt mixed loyalties when conflicts arose between the colonies and the mother country. But even the appointive governors faced important constraints on their power, the chief being that the legislatures held the purse strings.

Each legislature was comprised of two houses, upper (the Lords) and lower (the Commons), but only the lower house could initiate fiscal legislation. Members of the lower house were elected, and power gradually shifted to the lower house as the colonial legislatures strove to imitate the House of Commons in England. General elections also determined the members of the upper house in Connecticut and Rhode Island; elsewhere, members of the upper house were appointed in the same way as the governor.

The fact that the colonists generally held effective control of the legislatures not only established a climate of independence; it also granted considerable political freedom over a wide range of questions both local and, as regards the issuing of paper money, international. Especially in such larger matters the role of the governor was to initiate policies consistent with imperial designs and to veto any conflicting legislation. However, even his best efforts were foredoomed if he could not obtain appropriations for his projects from a stubborn, purse-holding legislature. The governor was totally dependent on the legislature for his salary (which was often in arrears), with the one exception of Virginia, where there was a permanent flow of revenue from a tax on tobacco exports. Consequently, although the Crown was represented (or underrepresented) in colonial government, the practical power in civil affairs typically rested with the colonists themselves, through their elected representatives.

The authority that permitted these conditions, of course, rested in England. The colonies were not formally independent or free. Before the shift in power in England from the Crown to Parliament in the late seventeenth century, the king had exercised direct authority over the colonies. After 1690, however, that authority gradually passed into the hands of Parliament, which, generally being preoccupied with other interests, rarely issued laws specifically directed toward the colonies. As a result, colonial affairs were typically assigned in Britain to two groups: the Board of Trade and Plantations, and the Privy Council. The board advised and acted as a conduit between the Secretary of State for the Southern Department and the colonial governors.

But directives from these bureaucracies were rare and, on occasion, they were simply ignored by the colonists, who considered them an impractical nuisance. Before 1763, then, bureaucratic apathy had in effect relinquished control, which the colonists were quick to grasp.

Despite this de facto assumption of power, the extent of local autonomy was officially limited. As a procedural matter, the Privy Council reviewed all laws passed in the colonies. In the process it vetoed a small portion of that legislation found to be in conflict with the interests of the empire; however, this only modestly reduced the degree of self-direction of colonists who were 3,000 miles and many months distant from the court of review. Because communication depended on slow-sailing ships, a law might be passed and long implemented in the colonies before it ever came up for review in England. And if, by some mischance, a popular piece of legislation happened to be vetoed in the homeland, it could simply be reworded and passed again.

Briefly put, the daily lives of most American colonists were influenced very little by British deliberations or, for that matter, by any legislation either in England or in the colonies. Government weighed relatively lightly in their affairs; and on the issues that most directly affected them, those of a local nature, the colonists themselves held the reins. It made little difference whether one was called an American colonist or a British subject; in fact if not in name, colonists enjoyed extensive freedom of self-determination.

Mercantilist restrictions before 1763

This apparent freedom rested, of course, on custom and common acceptance. Legally, the colonists were subject to severe constraints, especially in matters of external economic relations and foreign policy. As emphasized in Chapter 4, the prevailing mercantilist doctrine dictated that the empire should be strengthened in every possible way, including an induced inflow of gold and other precious metals, the attainment of self-sufficiency in production, and the encouragement in the colonies of essential industries, especially those related to the sinews of war, such as shipping and shipfitting.

During the seventeenth and early eighteenth centuries, these goals were embodied and promoted in a wide-ranging series of parliamentary Navigation Acts that covered a multitude of products and services from iron and shipping to hats. They produced an equally mixed bag of effects. The acts with greatest impact in the colonies were those passed in the mid-seventeenth century with the threefold aim of encouraging British (and colonial) shipping, controlling trade, and developing England as an entrepôt.

That these acts benefited the British empire at the expense of other European empires, most notably the highly efficient commercial and maritime Dutch, was an important side effect. Their overall impact on the mainland colonies, however, was ambivalent and mixed.

By way of review, it should be recalled that the Navigation Act of 1661, concerned with shipping, restricted all colonial trade to British (and colonial) vessels. A foreign ship could land goods in Britain, but only from the country of its registry, and not, say, from its own colonies or from other areas. To pass as "British" a ship had to be built and owned in the British empire and the crew had to be at least three-quarters British (or colonial); thus the highly efficient Dutch merchantmen were excluded from British colonial waters, to the obvious advantage of New Englanders both as shippers and as shipbuilders. On the other hand, groups like the southern tobacco farmers were burdened by higher freight rates because of the reduced supply of shipping services. Certain colonists gained, others lost; and the result is unclear.

Other acts, in 1660 and 1663, dealt with the flows of trade and directed that imports into the colonies from Continental Europe, with few exceptions had henceforth to be funneled through a British port. Only certain goods that Great Britain could not furnish, such as wine and salt, were exempted; these could be imported directly from Spain (but not from France). Other areas of the empire, such as from the British West Indies, were also allowed direct access to the mainland colonies. However, by all odds the largest share of trade into the colonies came either from or through Great Britain: on the eve of the American Revolution, England was the port of departure for 80 percent of colonial imports.

In addition, specific colonial products were now required to be shipped directly to Great Britain and landed there before being transshipped to their final destination. The list of such "enumerated articles" grew over time. It had begun with tobacco, sugar, indigo, dyewood, and cotton – mainly produce from the southern mainland and from the West Indies. By 1704 it was extended to include rice and molasses; between 1705 and 1729 various naval stores were added (pitch, tar, turpentine, masts, yards, and hemp); and in 1721 furs and skins were tacked on.

These trade distortions undoubtedly were burdensome to the American colonists, both raising the costs and reducing the flow of non-British imports. Similarly, the effect of channeling enumerated colonial commodities through Great Britain was to raise their shipping costs, to reduce the quantity demanded, and to lower profits for American exporters and producers of these products.

Granting, then, that these controls favored Britain at the expense of the colonies, one ought not to exaggerate the magnitude of the burden. Colonial items reexported from Britain received rebates on most, if not all, of the taxes collected there. The extra costs of handling and transshipment remained, but because of common blood and language, as well as a need for credit, colonists would in any case have shipped many of their goods (both exports and imports) through Britain. (We shall see in the following chapter that no great change appeared in the patterns of trade following the American Revolution. In fact, after the new nation had won the right to ship how and where it chose, the great bulk of American tobacco continued during the 1780s and 1790s to travel to Britain, even though most of it was destined for reexport to the Continent.)

To return, then, to the situation during colonial times: in some cases the colonists actually benefited directly through bounties paid on various favored items like indigo and certain naval stores. In other cases, where severe hardship developed, the regulations were relaxed to allow direct trade. This happened when the enumeration of rice had priced the American product out of Southern European markets; thereafter, direct shipment was permitted to ports south of Cape Finisterre (in northern Spain). Lastly, some colonists eased the pains of adjustment by resorting to smuggling, until in 1696 a system of admiralty courts was set up to correct the initial lax enforcement of the acts.

Obviously, British manufacturers enjoyed special advan-

tages in the American colonial market – but not wholly because the Navigation Acts imposed extra costs on competitive foreign products en route to the colonies. Natural
advantages also favored them over potential colonial manufacturers. On the one hand, the colonies were rich in supplies of the "trading goods" of agricultural and resource-
intensive products, and comparatively their advantage
centered on the production of these types of goods. In addition, the colonial population was so small and scattered as to
discourage large-scale, low-cost methods of production in
the colonies. Furthermore, the "natural tariff" normally
created by the cost of transportation was minimal in the case
of goods traveling westward across the Atlantic, because
comparative underutilization resulted in exceptionally low
freight rates. Thus the New World remained overwhelmingly dependent on the mother country for its supplies of
manufactured goods. Rarely indeed (primarily in the case of
shipbuilding) did colonial manufacture even remotely
threaten to compete with British interests.

Whenever such a possibility did loom, special-interest
groups in England were quick to stifle any challenge, real or
apparent, to their dominance. In 1669, for example, British
colonies were forbidden to produce woolens for export,
even to a neighboring colony. In fact, however, that enactment was directed against Ireland. American colonists, satis-
fied with their right to produce homespun for basic gar-
ments and bedding and for personal use or local trade, were
happy enough to obtain more refined woolen manufactures
from Britain at the lower cost made possible by large-scale
production methods in use there. That situation continued
even after independence was achieved; American woolens
were no match for imported British fabrics until the nineteenth century, when the combined effects of a war, an embargo, and legislated protective tariffs finally pried open the
local market for domestic woolens.

One small segment of colonial industry was hurt to a
somewhat greater extent by the Hat Act passed by Parlia-

ment in 1732. This one-sided legislation favored London hatters by prohibiting the export of beaver-fur hats produced primarily in New England and New York. Its effect on the overall American economy was negligible, however.

Similarly, Parliamentary restrictions relating to iron proved moderately harmless. Whereas colonial production of raw pig and bar iron was encouraged, the finishing of iron and steel, and the use of certain types of equipment, were forbidden after 1750. Nevertheless, the law was ignored with impunity, and despite the ease of detection twenty-five iron mills were established between 1750 and 1775 in Pennsylvania and Delaware alone. The effective freedom enjoyed by the colonists was further demonstrated when the Pennsylvania assembly appropriated financial aid to a new slitting mill (nail factory) in open defiance of the law.

Were these restrictions on colonial manufacturing primarily designed to serve the ends of British imperial policy? Granted, they did discourage competing economic activities. Moreover, they encouraged the production of raw materials to complement an industrializing Britain. But far more obviously, they were tailored to the special interests of groups with influence in Parliament; it is highly doubtful that the Hat Act, in particular, could be defended on mercantilist principles. The noteworthy fact is that no matter how distasteful these enactments were to the colonists, they were largely either superfluous (as with woolens), or ignored (as with slitting mills), or inconsequential (as with hat production). Indeed, their effects were largely invisible in the face of economic forces and comparative advantages in production.

There was one exceptional case, however, in which special interests succeeded in promoting legislation that had portentous implications for the American Revolution. Of all the enactments before 1763, the Molasses Act of 1733 hit the colonies hardest. Around the turn of the eighteenth century, British sugar planters in the British Caribbean islands had begun to lose ground to the increasingly efficient French. As the scales tipped, American colonists found that French sugar and molasses cost less than British. Moreover, whereas the market for colonial goods in the British islands showed only modest increases, the French islands offered an eager and expanding market. Not surprisingly, after 1700 American ships began to anchor more and more frequently in French ports, setting up a brisk trade from New England and the middle colonies. Meantime, however, British planters feeling the sting of French competition dispatched their lobbyists to demand protection from Parliament, which obliged in 1733 by clapping high duties onto all foreign sugar, molasses, and rum imported into the mainland colonies.

To impose those penalties was one thing; to enforce them quite another. The smuggling of French sugar promptly became the order of the day. The authorities had ample means of detecting such violations: the governors had been supplied with staffs for that purpose after 1675 and admiralty courts had been set up in 1696. But common sense dictated that officials look the other way because the potential burdens of the enactment on mainland colonies, especially on New England, were simply too great. A flourishing trade would have been reduced in both directions: not only would the colonists have paid higher prices for sugar, molasses, and rum but their exports of fish, lumber, and provisions would have brought less profit in a restricted market.

In short, serious repercussions were avoided in the northern mainland colonies only because a sensible "statutory neglect" became the accepted rule, and therein lay the prime significance of the Molasses Act of 1733. Since it was not enforced, it inflicted no serious economic damage. But for the first time a key act of Parliament was openly ignored by both colonists and British officials. An irreversible precedent had been set.

Three crises and revolt

Although the period of informal neglect and casual tolerance lasted for more than a century, it did not persist. It ended in 1763 with the close of the Seven Years' War or, as it was known in the colonies, the French and Indian War. Victorious Britain had finally and convincingly won the struggle for empire along the Atlantic shelf of North America. Ironically that elimination of French power played an important role in the coming of the American Revolution. For one thing, it removed an enemy held in common by both the American colonists and citizens of Britain. As a consequence, an important sense of common purpose was lost. In addition, the absence of the French greatly reduced the possibility that an American nation, truly independent of Britain, would be quickly overtaken by some other powerful political interest in North America. As a result, an important prop to colonial allegiance was pulled away.

The close of war left the British empire with other headaches beside the altered political climate of the colonies. The most urgent was the age-old question of funds. A costly and protracted struggle had so badly depleted the treasury that to reduce the national debt Parliament was forced to consider the politically unloved option of raising taxes. But where? The home front was already war-weary and tax-harassed. What about making the distant colonies share the cost of the war and of maintaining the peace? Despite their proximity to the battlefields, the colonists had never contributed heavily in either troops or matériel. Worse, many of them had notoriously engaged in profiteering; it was even charged that essential war supplies had been smuggled to the besieged French sugar colony of Saint-Dominique (now known as Haiti) so that British forces had failed to capture that prize. Such blatant ingratitude weighed heavily on the minds of Britons and fostered sentiment for colonial taxation.

Meantime, the colonists were busily stirring up more worries, and more expense, for the homeland. Almost before the Seven Years' War had ended, crowds of eager white settlers were pushing over the Appalachians and invading hitherto untouched Indian territory. Angered and fearful, the tribes retaliated with effective vigor under the leadership of Chief Pontiac, and destroyed seven out of nine garrisons west of Niagara before the uprising was finally quelled. To prevent further outbreak, in 1763 George III issued a royal proclamation that stifled movement into the trans-Appalachian West and put the fur trade under centralized control by requiring traders and trappers to obtain permission to cross the mountains. Similarly, governors' rights to dispose of far western lands were curtailed, and, such disposition henceforth required explicit permission from Britain.

Of course the Indian uprising further compounded the war costs left over from the French and British conflict. To reinforce the western and Canadian garrisons and secure the frontier, George Grenville, the English prime minister, had to station 10,000 British troops in the colonies at an estimated annual expense of nearly £350,000.

From the British viewpoint it seemed only fair that the Americans should pay at least a portion of these expenses. The hard financial facts also bore out this view. As Table 18 vividly shows, per-capita tax burdens in the mainland colonies shortly after the war were exceptionally low by compari-

Table 18. *Index of per-capita tax burdens in 1765 (Great Britain = 100)*

Great Britain	100
Ireland	26
Massachusetts	4
Connecticut	2
New York	3
Pennsylvania	4
Maryland	4
Virginia	2

Source: Derived from estimates by R. R. Palmer as given in Gerald Gunderson, *A New Economic History of America* (New York: McGraw-Hill Book Company, 1976), p. 89.

son to the burdens in Britain and Ireland. (Although there were differences in the average per-capita wealth holdings in Great Britain and in the colonies, these adjusted estimates adequately reveal the approximate comparative burdens based on ability to pay.) Clearly, colonial residents were carrying only a small fraction of the tax burdens of their fellow citizens of Britain.

Who had the greater ability to pay higher taxes, and who would benefit more from a secure western frontier? From the banks of the Thames the answer appeared clear enough, and Parliament passed two laws to help defray the expense of the American garrisons.

The first of these, the Sugar Act of 1764, was really little more than a refinement of the Molasses Act of 1733. Surprisingly it did not even raise existing taxes; in fact, the duties on imports of non-British West Indian products (sugar, molasses, and rum) were drastically reduced. For instance, the duty on French molasses was cut from sixpence per gallon to three pennies. The one great difference was that the law now included strict provisions for the collection of the tax. Secondarily it also tacked a few more items onto the list of enumerated articles, raised duties on select foreign textiles, and repealed the tariff rebates on foreign goods reexported from Britain to the colonies.

The decision to concentrate on Caribbean products as the objects of taxation was based on two considerations. First, they were so valuable that even a lowered tax rate would yield a good return if collection were strict; next, the law would pacify the British West Indian planters, who were still clamoring for protection from the foreign islands and from the growing competition of New England rum. Again, the voice of special interests was heeded in Parliament.[1] Although they were not used to strict enforcement, the American colonies were not opposed to such specialized taxes as a matter of principle. After all, they had lived for nearly a century with *external taxes* that were viewed as serving the ends of mercantile policy.

The second measure – the Stamp Act – was quite a different matter. Designed solely to raise money, this act required stamps of varying value to be affixed to specified documents, ranging from legal contracts and documents, through pamphlets and newspapers, to playing cards and dice. Here, then, was an "internal" tax that threatened to snatch the power of the purse away from the hands of colonial legislatures. American political territory had been invaded.

As these edicts were put to the test in the colonies, and as it became increasingly apparent that they were to be strictly enforced, a howl of outrage arose. In retrospect it is obvious that Grenville did not make the wisest selection of items to stamp. Articulate lawyers, some perhaps with political ambitions, loudly aired their grievances against the need for stamps on legal papers; and this anti-British chorus was broadcast far and wide by stamp-weary publishers of newspapers. "No taxation without representation" became the rallying cry of disgruntled colonists.

As they saw it, economic sanctions required economic reprisals. To develop a working counterattack, various colonial interests joined together in New York in 1765 to form a Stamp Act Congress. Several resolutions were passed, but by far the most important was a decision to boycott British goods. Nonimportation associations quickly sprang up as the boycott spread throughout the colonies. The impact on British imports was dramatic: docks and warehouses bulged with unsold British items, and shipments from Britain dwindled. As shown in Figure 15, between 1764 and 1766 the official value of imports tumbled in the middle colonies, where the boycott was centered and first organized, and sharp reductions also occurred in the upper South.[2] New England, however, was only a weak partner and the lower South apparently did not join in the boycott.

Overall, the nonimportation agreements were highly successful and the colonists were able to export some of the stamp crisis back to England. As trade dried up, British merchants and manufacturers joined sides with the colonists, pleading for reconsideration of the new taxes. In the spring of 1766 Parliament conceded: the Stamp Act was repealed, and duties on foreign molasses were lowered from three pennies to one penny per gallon. Once the crisis was resolved, British exports again shot briskly upward, as shown in Figure 15, despite some lingering minor irritations. One of these unhealed sore points was the Quartering Act of 1765, which required colonial assemblies to help finance barracks, provisions, and transport of British troops. Some sugar duties also remained. And as a face-saving addendum to the tax repeals, Parliament passed the Declaratory Act, which reasserted the right of Parliament to govern and to legislate for the American colonies. This was little more than a threat, however, and at the time caused scarcely a ripple among the colonists, who were more on guard against active and effective legislation than against assertions of the right to legislate.

Figure 15. Official values of British imports into the American colonies, 1763–75. *Source:* U. S. Bureau of the Census, *Historical Statistics of the United States, Colonial Times to 1957* (Washington, D.C.: Government Printing Office, 1960), p. 757.

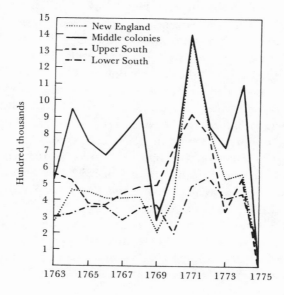

The calm following the first crisis was short-lived. A second brushfire flared up in 1767. In that year Charles Townshend, replacing Grenville as Chancellor of the Exchequer, decided to heed the persistent requests of British landowners to lighten property taxes. To recoup the lost revenues, he imposed duties on various colonial imports, such as tea, paper, paint, glass, and other items. Cleverly avoiding "internal" taxes on the colonies, he thus resorted only to imposts that were irksome but not economically burdensome and that took only a fraction of 1 percent of colonial incomes. What stung the highly independent colonists, however, was the manner of enforcement. Colonial courts were allowed to issue search warrants, known as writs of assistance; in addition, an American Customs Board was created, and vice-admiralty courts were established in Halifax, Boston, Philadelphia, and Charleston to handle smuggling cases.

The earlier boycott had taught the colonists an invaluable lesson in practical economics: North America had become an important market for British manufacturers and strong repercussions had shaken Britain when that market dried up. Indeed, by this time 25 percent of all British exports were destined for North America. So again the colonists responded with boycotts, which lasted from late 1768 into early 1770, with effects again vividly revealed in Figure 15. Trade plunged downward in all regions except the upper South, the only area spared the distasteful vice-admiralty courts.[3]

Once again British merchants hastily sent pleas to Parliament, and for a second time Parliament backed down. In the spring of 1770 the Townshend duties were repealed except that on tea. Trade was renewed, and in late 1770 and throughout 1771, English imports flooded into the colonies to satisfy pent-up demand. This upswing and an overextension of credit precipitated a sharp reversal in 1772, as displayed in Figure 15; but except for this business cycle, trade was reasonably normal.[4]

The colonists had won a second round. However, this time

the irritations left in the wake of the boycott were of greater substance. Perhaps the one event most responsible for arousing anti-British emotions, at least in New England, was the Boston Massacre in March 1770. British redcoats stationed in Boston, mainly to enforce customs regulations and to protect customs officials from occasional outbreaks of mob violence, were often themselves the victims of badgering and mob action.[5] Every form of intimidation was probably tried against them, including citizen arrests for walking on the grass of the Boston Commons.

The March incident began typically, but ended tragically: soldiers who had taken all they could stand of abuse, name calling, threats, and pelting with rocks and snowballs finally responded by shooting into the crowd that had gathered.[6] Sympathetic though we may feel toward the soldiers performing a thankless duty, there is no question that they acted without due provocation. No shots had been fired at them, yet they killed three persons outright, mortally wounded two others, and injured six more.

The colonists now had a rallying cry to stir the blood of their fellows. Nevertheless, satisfactory relations continued to prevail between Great Britain and its American colonies until 1773, when Parliament burst the calm with a piece of legislation in no way directly related to the colonies. Not unlike today, when the federal government sometimes comes to the rescue of large enterprises (serving at least nominally the public interest), Parliament sought to bail out the financially ailing British East India Company[7] with a loan and an enactment that changed the procedures of marketing tea. Prior to that time the company, which held a monopoly on British tea imports from the Far East, had been required to ship tea directly to Britain, from where it was exported to colonial wholesalers, who in turn sold it to retailers. Now, in permitting the British East India Company to ship directly to the colonies, the new act inadvertently sidestepped the colonial wholesaler. The price of tea in the colonies promptly fell by half, both because the British duty

was avoided and because handling and middleman costs
were reduced. However, the delighted consumers of tea
were outshouted by special-interest groups – mainly the in-
dignant wholesalers and the smugglers of Dutch tea[8] – who
argued that if one type of business could be destroyed by
Parliament all might be in equal peril. Businessmen, merchants, and shopkeepers were united and on the alert for
possible mischief by Parliament. Was colonial enterprise to
be sacrificed for the sake of powerful British monopolies?

It quickly became clear that Parliament had bungled into a
third crisis of unforeseen dimensions. Not surprisingly, old
tactics were put to work again: colonists in the major tea
ports of Boston, New York, Philadelphia, and Charleston
refused to handle the tea. Shipments from England piled up
or were returned. And Boston Harbor gained a place in
history when a band of rum-drinking colonists served British
high tea to the fish in the harbor. Such wanton destruction
of private property, amounting to tens of thousands of
pounds sterling, outraged many citizens even in the colonies,
but it served mainly to toughen the conviction in the homeland that something had to be done to bring those colonists
into line, or else Parliament could surrender all pretense to
authority.

The resultant punitive legislation came to be known with
descriptive accuracy as the Intolerable Acts. In the summer
of 1774 these acts (1) closed the port of Boston to all shipping until the East India Company was reimbursed for its
lost tea; (2) placed restrictions on town meetings in Massachusetts; (3) made council membership appointive (by the
Crown-appointed governor) rather than elective; (4) allowed
British officials accused of crimes in connection with the
performance of their duties to be tried in another colony or
in Britain, away from a locally hostile populace; and, of
course (5) stationed more troops there (at Boston's expense).

As the confrontation intensified, the colonists resorted to
economic sanctions for a third time. The First Continental
Congress assembled in Philadelphia in September and voted

a total embargo on trade with Britain and the British West Indies. As shown in Figure 15, the embargo was even more successful than its predecessors, but this time it came too late to effect a peaceful settlement. The confrontation had been pushed to ideological and political limits that could be resolved only on the battlefield. By April 1775 the battles of Lexington and Concord had set the colonies on an irreversible course toward independence. The third crisis, also, was destined to become a victory for the colonies, but only at the cost of a long, bloody war and of economic exhaustion.

Exploitation and the Revolution

It is sometimes alleged that the American Revolution resulted from the inevitable clash of competing capitalisms, from "a basic conflict between British mercantile policy on the one hand and the Northern colonial merchants' need for expansion on the other."[9] Taking this as a working hypothesis, let us consider strictly economic factors as they related to the revolt.

Were British restrictions hitting hard at the pocketbook of the average colonist or particular groups or regions? Did independence offer more promise for economic expansion than could be achieved within the empire? It is not likely that the second question can ever be satisfactorily answered. Only the short-run consequences of freedom can be meaningfully assessed – a task awaiting us in Chapter 9. However, we can attempt to measure the degree of *exploitation* in terms of costs to colonial income. Did the British regulations really impose significant economic hardship? Or did they simply chafe the sensibilities of colonists who had grown to cherish their long-assumed rights of self-determination?

There are four major areas of regulation to consider: manufacturing restraints, land policy, currency policy, and (most important) the acts related to trade. How much better off economically would the colonists have been without these British restrictions?

As we have already suggested, manufacturing restrictions were few and of negligible importance. Of those governing the production of wool for export, finished iron, and beaver hats, only the latter imposed any significant individual burdens, and that on a small group long since accustomed and adjusted to the restraint. As a percentage of national income, the total of these burdens was infinitesimal, and the course of manufacturing development in the colonies was affected very little by British restrictions. For the most part they were unnecessary, because manufacturing activity was automatically limited by the scattered and small size of colonial markets and by the colonies' overwhelming comparative advantage in agriculture and in resource-intensive products. Consequently, although manufacturing restrictions offered a tempting medium of exploitation, the legislation actually adopted had literally no effect on aggregate income in the colonies.

As to British land policy, its generally liberal nature, designed to encourage rapid development, has already been noted. This policy was sharply reversed following the Indian uprising and war with Chief Pontiac. However, the resulting royal proclamation of 1763 that set boundaries of legal settlement left them somewhat flexible, and the line shifted westward in 1768, after certain Indian treaties made large tracts available to settlers and speculators. Controls were again tightened by the Quebec Act of 1774. By virtue of this (one of the Intolerable Acts), western lands claimed by Massachusetts, Connecticut, and Virginia were redistributed to the province of Quebec, and the terms by which land could pass into private hands were made more stringent. In addition, territorial governments were now to be entirely in the hands of royal officials, and it was stipulated that trials there were to be without juries.

Although the political implications are clear enough, the economic consequences of the newly restrictive land policies remain unclear. Potential settlers in the West were made worse off, and land as a resource was made less available to all. Farmers in the older established areas, however, were possibly spared a degree of competition from western farmers, and land in the East probably gained in value. Overall, the restrictions probably reduced colonial incomes somewhat, because less land was made available for productive use. On the other hand, were the restrictions a matter of necessity because of the Indian population in the West?

Perhaps the most reliable evidence suggesting that these land policies were either not economically burdensome or were a matter of necessity is that the same basic restraints were prescribed and adopted by the federal government after independence. It seems unlikely that the new government would have adopted them if they could have been avoided or if they weighed heavily on the American people.

The same thing is true in the sense of restrictions on currency issues: after independence was achieved, the new government adopted measures very similar to those that had earlier been imposed by Britain. To look at the background: in 1751, Parliament had passed a Currency Act that prohibited New England from adding new land banks (concentrating in loans for land purchase) and from issuing more paper money. The act did weigh against debtors in that area, and the relative burden was demonstrated by colonial reaction to a supplemental Restraining Act in 1764. At that time the colonies, especially the Chesapeake area, had gone heavily in debt to British merchants because they had continued to import goods from Britain during the Seven Years' War although their own exports to the mother country had dwindled. To boost its depressed economy, Virginia issued £250,000 in bills of credit. British creditors now stood to lose because the planters could repay with cheap money the debts they had built up in hard sterling, and a sharp answer came from Britain in the form of an extension of the original Currency Act to cover all colonies. The enactment undoubtedly hurt the hard-pressed Chesapeake region and perhaps explains the unusual support given by the upper South to the boycott of British goods in 1765. But the adoption of similar controls after independence attests that the economic burden could not have been oppressive overall and that the real point at issue was simply whether Britain, or the colonists themselves, should hold the reins of monetary control.

Not so with the Acts of Trade. Although recent investigators[10] are one in their conclusion that the economic burden of regulations on land, currency, and manufacturing was trivial, they do agree that the Acts of Trade did exploit the colonies. In Lawrence Harper's words,

> The enumeration of key colonial exports in various Acts from 1660 to 1766 and the Staple Act of 1663 hit at colonial trade both coming and going. The Acts required the colonies to allow English middlemen to distribute such crops as tobacco and rice and stipulated that if the colonies would not buy English manufacturers, at least they should purchase their European goods in England. The greatest element in the burden laid upon the colonies was not the taxes assessed. It consisted in the increased costs of shipment, trans-shipment, and middleman's profits arising out of the requirement that England be used as an entrepôt.[11]

Harper was the first scholar to attempt to quantify the burdens that resulted from forced indirect routing of colonial trade. A host of others – Thomas, McClelland, Ransom, and Walton among them – have followed his trailblazing studies with refinements and modifications resulting from the unearthing of better and more complete data and from improved techniques of measurement.

The procedures for estimating the burdens are tedious exercises that need not be repeated here. It will suffice to outline the basic principles involved and to report the findings. Essentially, the problem boils down to the adjustment of prices and quantities on goods traded through Britain. How much higher would prices have been in the colonies on colonial goods shipped to the Continent via Britain had direct trade been allowed? How much larger would the quantity of such exports have been? Contrarily, how much less might colonists have paid for their imports, given direct shipments (recall the effect on tea prices in 1774), and how much more might they have imported?

Using the postwar period as a guide to changes in relative prices and other market adjustments, multiple separate and independent investigations (referred to in note 10) concur that the maximum amount of exploitation from the Acts of Trade was between 1 and 3 percent of colonial national income, with 1 percent or less being the more acceptable estimate.

Of course, 1 percent is not trivial; moreover, the heaviest burdens from enumerations fell on one region, the upper South, and there the average income loss was probably around 2.5 percent.[12] Alternatively, the other burdens were more evenly spread, such as those stemming from import restrictions that fell on individuals approximately in proportion to their import expenditures. But the acts also yielded bounties and other benefits; and membership in the empire included the advantages of British naval protection and a free trading realm. After independence the colonists painfully learned that these had been no trifling considerations. When weighed in the scales, they reduced the burdens of regulation to insignificant proportions.

Most scholars agree with Dickerson, therefore, that the Navigation Acts were not an important element in the thrust for independence. Gray maintains that even those hardest hit – the tobacco interests – had fully adjusted to them:

> After the industry had become thoroughly adjusted to these restrictions it is doubtful if they bore severely on colonial producers, and . . . there is little official opposition by the tobacco colonies to the Navigation Acts.
>
> In short while British policy was formulated with a view to appropriating the golden egg made available by . . . the tobacco trade . . . it was careful to nourish and sustain the colonial goose.[13]

Similarly, Harper points out that

> Anyone who maintains that the Revolution resulted
> from the inevitable clash of competing capitalisms must
> reckon with several points: That burdens upon the
> trans-Atlantic trade were proportionately greater at the
> beginning of the eighteenth century than in 1776; that
> the restraints of the land and currency policies were
> basically the same as those prescribed by the federal
> government; and that after 1766 the taxes laid on mo-
> lasses by Britain were less than those imposed by the
> United States after 1790.[14]

Finally, the restraints on trade were almost never listed by
the tobacco planters of the Chesapeake area in their list of
grievances against the mother country and the Acts of Trade
are not even mentioned in the Declaration of Independence.
Overall, the case for economic exploitation as a main force
spurring the colonists toward revolt is extremely weak, too
weak to deserve more than passing notice.

Conclusion

Rather than economic exploitation it was the introduction of
new rules to the game after 1763 that precipitated the
American Revolution. Before 1763, the colonists had been
happily neglected and free to do pretty much as they
pleased, interrupted only on occasion by a new enactment or
a veto of some piece of colonial legislation. But suddenly,
and acceleratingly, the colonists found themselves the recipi-
ents of all kinds of unwelcome attention. A host of new
regulations descended on them; worse, the rules were to be
enforced. Almost everyone could find a grievance: debtors
had the Currency Act; frontiersmen and political radicals
had the Quebec Act; politicians, printers, and gamblers, the
Stamp Act; tea merchants and smugglers, the Tea Act. Re-
sentments flared everywhere, fired through Committees of
Correspondence and other groups of agitators, calling

loudly on their fellows to claim formally the rights they had long held de facto.

American independence had become inevitable. But that is not to say the American Revolution was equally inevitable. Other English colonies have subsequently gained independence without such drastic measures. Charles Andrews has pointed out that the political and economic development of the mainland colonies had reached a point where they

> qualified to co-operate with the mother country on terms similar to those of a brotherhood of free nations such as the British world is becoming today [1926]. But England was unable to see this fact, or to recognize it, and consequently America became the scene of a political unrest which might have been controlled by a compromise, but was turned to revolt by coercion. The situation is a very interesting one, for England is famous for her ability to compromise at critical times in her history. For once at least she failed.[15]

The nature of that "failure" is nicely summarized by Harper:

> As a mother country, Britain had much to learn. Any modern parents' magazine could have told George III's ministers that the one mistake not to make is to take a stand and then to yield to howls of anguish. It was a mistake which the British government made repeatedly. It placed a duty of 3d. per gallon on molasses, and when it encountered opposition, reduced it to 1d. It provided for a Stamp Act and withdrew it in the face of temper tantrums. It provided for external taxes to meet the colonial objections and then yielded again by removing all except one. When finally it attempted to enforce discipline it was too late. Under the circumstances, no self-respecting child – or colonist – would be willing to yield.[16]

Perhaps those lessons served the British well in later periods when others of their colonies made the transition to independence without resort to revolution.

Glossary of terms

Exploitation
Economic exploitation is a situation in which a nation precludes another nation, or colony, from achieving as much in return from its economic activities as it would have had the interference not occurred. Generally, it is viewed as a situation where the exploited nation or colony does not achieve as much income as it contributes to output.

External taxes
Taxes and duties levied on commodities exchanged between the colonies and overseas areas.

Selected readings

Dickerson, Oliver, *The Navigation Acts and the American Revolution* (Philadelphia: University of Pennsylvania Press, 1951).

Harper, Lawrence A., "Mercantilism and the American Revolution," *Canadian Historical Review*, XXIII (1942), pp. 1–15.

"The Effect of the Navigation Acts on the Thirteen Colonies," in Richard B. Morris (ed.), *The Era of the American Revolution* (New York: Columbia University Press, 1939; reprinted by Harper Torchbooks, 1965), pp. 3–39.

Hughes, Jonathan R.T., "Discussion," *American Economic Review*, LIX (1969), pp. 382–4.

Krooss, Herman E., "Discussion," *American Economic Review*, LIX (1969), pp. 384–5.

McClelland, Peter D., "The Cost to America of British Imperial Policy," *American Economic Review*, LIX (1969), pp. 370–81.

"On Navigating the Navigation Acts with Peter D. McClelland: A Reply," *American Economic Review*, LX (1970), pp. 956–8.

Price, Jacob, "Discussion," *Journal of Economic History*, XXV (1965), pp. 655–9.

Ransom, Roger, "British Policy and Colonial Growth: Some Implications of the Burden from the Navigation Acts," *Journal of Economic History*, XXVIII, 3 (September 1968), pp. 427–35.

Reid, Joseph D., Jr., "On Navigating the Navigation Acts with Peter D. McClelland: Comment," *American Economic Review*, LX (1970), pp. 949–55.

Thomas, Robert P., "A Quantitative Approach to the Study of the Effects of British Imperial Policy upon Colonial Welfare: Some Preliminary Findings," *Journal of Economic History*, XXV (1965), pp. 615–38.

"British Imperial Policy and the Economic Interpretation of the American Revolution," *Journal of Economic History*, XXVII, 3 (September 1968), pp. 436–40.

Walton, Gary M., "The New Economic History and the Burdens of the Navigation Acts," *Economic History Review*, 2nd ser., XXIV (1971), pp. 533–42.

Economic prospects for the new republic

Not surprisingly, the Revolution brought about widespread disorder to the economy of North America. We have already seen how the three periods of nonimportation agreements disrupted trade and production in the late colonial years. The war itself played much greater havoc, stifling trade and upsetting the normal peacetime use of resources. Prior to the war, the colonists had increasingly depended upon trade with overseas markets to lift themselves above levels of mere subsistence. Now they were thrown back on their own resources, and economic efficiency ebbed with the curtailment of that specialization made possible by overseas shipping and trade.

Wartime commerce, 1775–82

Indirect and qualitative evidence permits a rough sketch of the new magnitudes and patterns of trade that took shape during the war.

Legal restrictions implemented in 1775 by both the British and the Americans immediately ended all direct and legal trade between the revolting colonies and Great Britain and the British West Indies. Since this had constituted the major portion of total colonial trade, the effects were prompt and drastic. Among other results, the halting of legal trade invited smuggling: even British goods, often disguised as non-British, crept into the colonies by devious routes through the Caribbean, Continental Europe, and Nova Scotia. The colonies profited to some extent from the capture of prizes, which approached 2,000 British ships and exceeded America's total naval losses. Nevertheless, to the colonies the net gain from privateering was small, and even when combined with clandestine activities it only partly offset the lack of imports.

The corresponding loss of American exports to Britain and her loyal American possessions was equally demoralizing. The elimination of bounties on certain southern staples – principally indigo and naval stores – and the sharp increase in freight rates, together with the British blockade of many major American ports, increased the pressures of the American trade embargo.

By mid-1775 shortages had already developed for such everyday items as salt, shoes, woolens, and linens; even more acute was the need for war-related goods like gunpowder, flints, muskets, and knives. To procure arms and ammunition, Congress late in 1775 authorized limited trade with the non-British West Indies; by the following spring, restrictions on trade to any foreign area were lifted. France, Spain, and Holland, together with their American possessions, became important trading partners of the revolting colonies. Although these new patterns of commerce partly offset the decline in trade with Britain, they were inadequate, even when combined with smuggling and the gains from privateering, to compensate fully for the loss of the legal British trade.

Moving in tandem with the changing fortunes of war, the levels of wartime trade reached their nadir in 1776 and 1777, the years in which the British maintained an effective though incomplete naval blockade of American ports. The main ports from southern New England to Philadelphia were blockaded for most of the war, especially before 1778. When the noose around Boston was loosened after mid-1776, that port became a stronghold of American trade and privateering for the duration of the war. The southern ports were kept open, off and on, until Savannah was taken in

December 1778 and Charleston in May 1780, but they saw little activity until commercial bonds with Europe were strengthened. Although some trade continued even at British-occupied ports such as New York, the volume was petty, especially for exports.

From their casual early policy of open ports to foreigners, the American colonies now began to negotiate formal treaties of commerce. The first such alliance was with France in 1778, and from this date until early 1782 American wartime commerce was at its zenith. Paralleling and reinforcing the rise of French-American commerce was the growth of trade with Spain and Holland, especially after those nations entered the war against Britain in 1779 and 1780, respectively.

The Dutch quickly became so active in carrying tobacco from the Chesapeake area that their island of St. Eustatius took on the characteristics of an entrepôt in the Caribbean. In fact, that lively trade hastened Britain's decision to declare war against Holland late in 1780. Although on a reduced level, prewar commercial contacts between New England and Spain were maintained throughout the war, especially the trade in fish, salt, and wine. Spain served also as a center for the sale of prizes captured by American privateers, and Spanish Cuba (like Holland's St. Eustatius) became an important trade center in the Caribbean, especially popular with Philadelphia and Baltimore merchants. Piqued by all this development, Britain deployed the Royal Navy southward into the Caribbean. St. Eustatius was seized in 1781, and in the next year the revolting colonies suffered such enormous shipping losses at sea that insurance costs and risks soared to all-time highs.

It is safe to assume, therefore, that the wartime flow of goods in and out of the colonies reached a peak before 1782, although even then it remained below prewar levels. Records on slave imports strongly point this way, as does substantial other evidence, albeit indirect. For example, it is known that earlier periods of conflict in North America sharply reduced commerce, particularly in exports. During the five years of hostilities that followed 1755, the official values of colonial exports had plummeted more than 40 percent below their 1751–5 levels even in the absence of legal restrictions or blockades. Obviously, the military and legal sanctions of the revolutionary period would have curbed the flow of trade even more sharply. In addition, the risks and costs of shipping were now higher and ships were fewer: not only had colonial ships been diverted into war service and privateering, but the British ships that once had carried the bulk of southern staples were about sterner business. The newcomer ships flying French, Dutch, and Spanish flags could only partly compensate for such losses.

Within the colonies, production for export was dried up by a number of additional factors. Colonial ships could no longer be sold to Britain. Bounties for specific colonial products had disappeared. Even the coastal trade was hampered by the lack of ships, by blockades, and by local embargoes imposed by individual colonies. Moreover, the sharp rise in ocean freight rates hit hardest at exports, which were typically of lower value relative to their bulk than were imports.

At another level, even business contracts were harder to negotiate, and far more costly, because of the uncertainties brought about by the *hyperinflation* of wartime finance. The general level of prices in the colonies rose at an unprecedented rate, increasing several hundred times from the beginning of the war to the withdrawal of Continental currency and the return to hard money in 1781.

These negative influences on American trade curtailed the amount of foreign exchange earned by the colonies from exports. On the other hand, military expenditures in the colonies by the French and the British, plus subsidies and loans from foreign governments, provided some means of payment for imports. On balance, however, the loss of short-term credit from British merchants and the higher costs of trade served to curtail the level of imports into the colonies to such an extent that foreign exchange accumulated. The net result was the channeling of American resources into industries that competed with imports and an increase in the economic self-sufficiency of the thirteen colonies. Examples of such adjustments abound. For instance, Bezanson, noting the increase of artisan workshops in and around Philadelphia, also states that the *putting-out system* became general early in the war, especially in spinning for the textile plants. By the middle of 1776, 4,000 women were employed in their homes under this system in the environs of Philadelphia alone.[1] Cereals put to use in making beer, whiskey, and other alcoholic beverages lessened the need either to import wines and West Indies rum or to import molasses for the domestic manufacture of rum.

In short, the stringencies of wartime were a mixed blessing for the colonies. On the one hand, they hastened the process of growing up, shifting young America from dependence on its motherland. On the other hand, the sharp curtailment of trade was an economic and social hardship, as witnessed (once more) by the torrent of imports that swept into North America, especially from Britain, once the trade lanes reopened with the coming of peace.

Peacetime: economic change in the short run

Peacetime opened a whole new era for North America. The difference, of course, lay in the one key word: independence. Economic adjustments had been relatively simple after earlier periods of hostilities because the rules were still the same: the colonies remained members of the empire. But in 1783, the young nation found itself outside the walls of the family that once had granted it bounties, privileges, and favored trade status. Moreover, even the wartime trade alliances with France and Spain were crumbling, as special privileges were withdrawn and tariffs and trade prohibitions reinstituted. If the 1760s and 1770s had presented crucial political decisions, the 1780s challenged America with equally critical economic problems. Its overseas trade was hobbled by drastic new restrictions. It faced an unknown future in market negotiations. Even the incipient manufacturing base that had taken root in the colonies under the impulse of wartime high prices was threatened now by the postwar floodtide of British imports.

In the Caribbean, American ships were excluded from direct trade with the British West Indies, and American merchantmen who tried to evade the restraints were subject to seizure by officials. Spain compounded the difficulty by withdrawing the wartime privilege of direct American trade with Cuba, Puerto Rico, and Hispaniola, while restating its traditional policy that its possessions were to import goods only from Spain. Only with the French West Indies was it possible to increase trade, but this did not suffice to compensate for the other losses of American shipping activity in the Caribbean. Even in the lively French trade, American shippers were not allowed to carry French sugar from the islands, and only in times of severe scarcity could the islands import American flour. In addition, American salted fish and meat were banned entirely from the British islands and subjected to high duties in the French.

Restrictions and trade curtailments were also felt in other waters. Because Americans were cut off from direct trade with the British fishery at Newfoundland, New England suffered a loss of commerce to the north in provisions, lumber, rum, and shipping services. To the east and into the Mediterranean, American shipping, which had been protected by the British flag and by British tribute to the governments of Tunis, Algeria, and Tripoli, now became fair game for the harassment of Barbary pirates.

Until new markets could be established, much of American shipping rocked at anchor. Predictably, American shipbuilding was also stifled, together with the supporting industries of lumber and naval stores. Out of postwar antagonism Britain now labeled as foreign all American-built vessels, which therefore were not eligible for trade within the empire even when owned by British subjects. This change of status resulted in the loss of a major market for American shipbuilders. Ship production was further deadened by the decline of American whaling, which had lapsed during the war and which never recovered because of prohibitive British duties imposed on American whale oil in 1783. In brief, the major American activities that employed American-built ships (cod fishing, whaling, and mercantile shipping) all were depressed. Since New England was the heartland of such activity, the region suffered disproportionately in the short run.

Other areas felt the woes of the same decline to a lesser extent. Pennsylvania and its neighboring states shared a loss in shipbuilding as well as in their commerce in wheat, flour, salted meat, and other provisions, especially to the West Indies. The region also had problems of its own. The specie accumulated during the war had been quickly spent on imports during the first two years of peace. At the end of that time, credit terms in England had tightened to such a degree that the imports were sharply restricted. By 1786 the middle Atlantic region had probably reached the bottom of a fairly severe business cycle. After the mid-1780s, conditions began to improve, as middle-colonial products were newly accepted into the traditional West Indian and Southern European markets.

In the South, the situation was mixed but in some ways even worse. British duties on rice restricted lower Southern planters to the markets of the West Indies and Southern Europe; as a result, the price of rice tumbled. The loss of bounties and subsidies on indigo and naval stores imposed further setbacks. Given little flexibility in its productive capacity (that is, the fact that alternative uses of its resources were so limited), the lower South faced more than a short-term crisis. In general, the markets for its products were not expanding, and its economic future did not look bright.

The upper South faced a similar problem because of a stagnant market for its major staple – tobacco. On the one hand Britain imposed a tax of fifteen pennies a pound on foreign tobacco. On the other, France granted monopoly rights to a single purchasing monopoly, the Farmers-General, for tobacco imports into France, whereas Spain and Portugal simply prohibited imports of American tobacco. Europeans might have wanted to fill their pipes with good American tobacco, but getting hold of it was an expensive matter.

One bright spot appeared in the otherwise clouded economic sky of the new nation. Goods that previously had been "enumerated" for transshipment through Britain might now be traded directly from American to European ports. Because shipping and handling costs were thus drastically lowered, many items shipped from America could command higher prices and higher profit margins. Indeed, one of the few economic barometers signaling recovery was the improving *terms of trade:* the relation of prices paid nationally for imports relative to prices received nationally for exports. By 1783, import prices were slightly below their prewar level on average, and export prices were higher. That year and 1784 brought the most favorable terms of trade. Thereafter they worsened until, by the later 1780s, there was little advantage to be seen over the prewar period.

A lack of quantitative evidence precludes a more precise measure of the new nation's economic problems, especially for the economy as a whole. Incomplete evidence on exports from two states, however, is available for 1784–92;[2] Table 19 shows this decline, then recovery in the mid- to late 1780s.

Table 19. *Exports from two states, 1784–92 (millions of dollars)*

	Pennsylvania	South Carolina
1784	3.7	2.1
1785	2.5	1.9
1786	2.1	2.3
1787	2.1	2.7
1788	2.4	2.6
1789–90	3.5	—
1790–2	3.4	2.7
1791–2	3.8	2.4

Reconsidered in terms of population growth, which was substantial over these postwar years, the estimates show that exports from Pennsylvania and South Carolina were expanding less rapidly than was the population during the period of Confederation. In other words, the relative importance of exports in these two states was clearly declining during the turbulent years of the 1780s. New Hampshire experienced sharp declines due to the depressed shipbuilding, fishing, and lumbering industries; elsewhere the economic picture cannot be determined.

At a time when the young nation was coming to grips with new economic realities it also faced a need to fill the governmental vacuum left by the departing British. As a result the political arena was as lively, and fully as chaotic, as the economic one.

Political and economic interaction

One of America's first and most influential economic managers, Alexander Hamilton, was a major voice for change and a powerful advocate for a strong central government. Expressing his displeasure with conditions under the Articles of Confederation – and not without some prejudice – he described the plight of the economy before the adoption of the Constitution:

> We may indeed with propriety be said to have reached almost the last stage of national humiliation. . . . Do we owe debts to foreigners and to our own citizens? . . . These remain without any proper provision for discharge. . . . Are we in a condition to repel aggression? . . . We have neither troops, nor treasury, nor government. . . . Are we entitled by nature and compact to the navigation of the Mississippi? Spain excludes us from it . . . Is commerce of importance to national wealth? . . . Ours is at the lowest point of declension.[3]

Foremost among the difficulties of the new nation was the problem of raising revenues: to fund the administration of government, to pay soldiers for benefits promised during the war, to pay for ships and troops to thwart piracy against American ships in the Mediterranean, to enforce law and order generally, and above all to fund the sizable national debt stemming from the war. Under the Articles of Confederation the power to tax was limited to the states, which understandably failed to raise revenues adequate for such national goals. Each state was quite willing to leave it to others to offer contributions to the central government, since the benefits of law and order and of debt repayment at the national level bore no direct relation to a given state's contribution.

The adoption of the Constitution changed all that. The power to tax was now delegated firmly to the central government, which was authorized to settle debts from the past – even those incurred by individual states. Events, of course, have abundantly demonstrated the wisdom of this course. Although there have been exceptions, generally the assurance that public debts will be honored has been a cornerstone in the development of a sound capital market in the United States. On the international level, it has undergirded negotiations for commodity exchanges and credit. And in private transactions, governmental responsibility in maintaining the confidence of investors has set an example for the faithful discharge of obligations.

Another constitutional provision that greatly improved the capital market was the assignment to the central government of the sole right to mint coinage and to regulate the money supply. A sound currency and a stable monetary system are crucial to the economic health of a nation, both as a medium of exchange to stimulate and to aid economic transaction and also as a medium for the holding of wealth. To the erstwhile colonists who had just emerged from monetary chaos and hyperinflation, a stable dollar represented a longed-for goal and one answer to the conflicting interests of creditors and debtors.[4]

One more matter of great political and economic significance was the question of who should regulate trade among the states. No substantial barriers to interstate commerce developed during the 1780s; however, the possibility of such barriers loomed as a threat until the Constitution specifically granted the regulation of interstate commerce to the federal government. States were now forbidden to erect tariffs to protect provincial interests, and a toll-free movement of goods was ensured. Such centralizing of power not only encouraged the growth of a national market but, in later decades, permitted the extension of federal authority to many areas of economic activity.

In addition, the federal government was given authority over foreign affairs, both for negotiating treaties and for setting tariffs. Competition among states to attract trade had formerly led to a tariff structure that, from the national perspective, was too low. However, as tariffs became part of federal policy-making, they were initially regarded less as a device to protect domestic industry than as a source of revenue. In fact, for most of early United States history they were the chief source of tax revenue. The power to regulate tariffs also handed to the federal government a powerful lever in negotiations to reduce or to eliminate duties on American goods abroad.[5]

In its effort to overcome the many short-run difficulties, and with an eye to long-term development, the newly independent republic made continual economic and political adjustments under its constitution. Perhaps the most important were those changes that strengthened the framework for protection of private property and enforcement of contracts. A climate of legal and political stability is critical to the formation of favorable economic conditions and it is not at all surprising that the short-run setbacks of the 1780s occurred. They simply accompanied a period of turbulence when the economy was straining to reorient itself and to develop new institutions and directions.

Americans had experienced better times, but in those years of struggle their future was brighter than their contemporaries could have anticipated. Different regions re-

covered at varying rates, but for that picture, we must turn
to a larger time span.

The longer-run perspective

The new American government began to collect customs
data in August of 1789. With this evidence, the foreign commerce for the years 1790–2 can be compared with that of
1768–72 and a systematic picture of trade alterations begins
to emerge. In fact, the eighteen-year interval between these
records actually gives needed perspective to observe the
longer-run effects of independence. Of course some of the
changes to be noted were simply a continuation of the shifting patterns of trade that had characterized the prerevolu-
tionary period. The West Indian trade, for example, had
been increasing in relative importance throughout the entire
eighteenth century. Consequently, though independence
was a powerful factor in altering trade patterns and magnitudes, it is impossible to isolate the impact of independence
from earlier trends and from changes that would have occurred had the thirteen colonies remained within the British
empire.

The adoption of the Constitution in 1789 and the gradual emergence of a stronger central government could have
had only a minimal impact on the economic structure and
activity of the states by the early 1790s. At that early date
the economy was still a product of the structure that had
existed before the Revolution, except as it had become
modified by the very fact of independence and by the read-
justments and such recovery as had taken place in the
1780s. Beginning in 1793, however, the entire situation
changed with the entry of the major European powers into
the Napoleonic Wars. As emphasized in Chapter 1, the resultant demand for United States exports and shipping
caused such a boom in American foreign trade as to over-
shadow completely any changes which could be attributed
to the Revolution itself or to independence.

To begin this comparison of American overseas trade, we see in Table 20 the annual average values of exports from the thirteen colonies to major overseas areas in 1768–72 compared with those from the United States in 1790–92. To make the data comparable, the dollar values from 1790–2 have been converted to sterling and 1768–72 prices.

Table 20. *Average annual real exports to overseas areas: the thirteen colonies, 1768–72, and the United States, 1790–2 (thousands of £; 1768–72 prices)*

Destination[a]	1768–72	Percentage of total	1790–2	Percentage of total
Great Britain and Ireland	1,616	58	1,234	31
Northern Europe			643	16
Southern Europe	406	14	557	14
British West Indies	759	27	402	10
Foreign West Indies			956	24
Africa	21	1	42	1
Canadian colonies			60	2
Other			59	1
Total	2,802	100	3,953	100

[a] Northern Europe includes Continental European countries north of Cape Finisterre. Southern Europe includes Spain, the Canary Islands, Portugal, Madeira, the Azores, the Cape Verde Islands, Gibraltar, and other Mediterranean ports in Europe (except French ports). The foreign West Indies include the Swedish, Danish, Dutch, French, and Spanish Caribbean possessions, and Florida and Louisiana. Africa includes North Africa, the west coast of Africa, and the Cape of Good Hope. The Canadian colonies include the British American colonies, including Newfoundland and the British fisheries; and St. Pierre, Miquelon, and the French fisheries. Other destinations include the East Indies, the northwest coast of America, and unidentified destinations.
Source: James F. Shepherd and Gary M. Walton, "Economic Change after the American Revolution: Pre- and Post-War Comparisons of Maritime Shipping and Trade," *Explorations in Economic History*, XIII (1976), p. 406.

From the table it is clear that by 1790 the United States had taken advantage of its new freedom to trade directly with other Northern European countries. The greater part of this trade was with France and the Netherlands, and the major commodity exported was tobacco, although rice, flour, wheat and corn were also in demand. The emergence of this brisk northern trade must be attributed to independence. Nevertheless, it is a somewhat puzzling fact that the lion's share of American exports reverted to Great Britain, in a trend that seems to have begun soon after the war ended (although prewar levels of exports to Britain had not yet been reached by 1790–2). Historians have speculated on the reasons for this renewal of loyalties. Part of the explanation may be that many of the imports for which Americans hungered were to be found in greatest variety and at the best price and quality there. British woolens, Irish linens, and the vast array of hardwares of British manufacture are examples. British merchants, too, enjoyed the advantages of a common language, established contacts, and a knowledge of American markets, and could thus regain a competitive edge over French and Dutch merchants after the war.

Meantime, by 1790 trade with the West Indies had surpassed its relative prewar role, and the war-disrupted trade with Southern Europe had recovered its relative position. The principal postwar shift in trade patterns cannot be shown in Table 20 because no precise breakdown is available between exports to the British and to the foreign West Indies for 1768–72. Before the Revolution, trade with the British West Indies had been greater than with the foreign islands. By 1790 the situation was reversed, largely because of the exclusion of American shipping from the British islands following the war. Undoubtedly this shift is overstated by the statistics, since many American ships clearing for foreign islands went illegally to British Caribbean areas; also, in the 1780s St. Eustatius remained an entrepôt from which British islands were supplied, as they had been during the war. Consequently, any conclusions about changes in the important West Indian trade brought about by independence must be tentative. It would appear, however, that although the war, and independence, must have played a part in the shift of United States trade toward non-British areas of the Caribbean, this trend had been set in motion before the Revolution and was probably only accelerated by the postwar restrictions on American shipping.

The changes in patterns of trade were accompanied by changes in the goods traded, as can be seen in Table 21. Not all commodity exports are listed, but those that composed the largest portion of exports are given (over 88 percent in 1768–72, and over 85 percent in 1790–2). Contrary to popular belief, the great prewar staple, tobacco, was no longer the single most valuable export by the early 1790s, although its export expanded beyond prewar levels.[6] (In fact, tobacco production may have equalled or perhaps exceeded prewar levels as early as the mid-1780s.[7]) Higher prices for tobacco in the 1780s, together with higher levels of output, resulted in modest recovery in the tobacco-producing areas of Virginia and Maryland and helped spread its cultivation into the piedmont region of North Carolina. No such good fortune touched the other important southern staples of rice and indigo, however, and the lower South lapsed into more of a self-subsistence economy in the 1780s. As time passed, the rising prices for rice offset the diminishing quantity exported, but for indigo both quantity and value had fallen by 1790. This decline may be attributed to the loss of the bounty and to increased British production of indigo in the West Indies after the war; however, the fall was not to drastically low levels, as some have stated.[8] Another commodity produced largely in the southern colonies was the large category of supplies known as naval stores. Their average annual export in 1790–2 was mixed, as compared with 1768–72, but their total value remained about the same and was small in both periods, relative to the "big three" of tobacco, rice, and indigo. Though average yearly exports of cotton had increased between

1768–72 and 1790–2, that crop was relatively unimportant before Whitney's invention of the cotton gin in 1793.

The striking feature of Table 21 is the increase in the export of foodstuffs like salted meats (beef and pork), bread and flour, corn, and wheat. Since these were essential elements in the West Indian trade, their increase during the postwar period should come as no surprise. What is more significant, however, is that the uptrend in food shipments to the West Indies was so well underway before the Revolution that the upper South was already shifting to grain production late in the colonial period. Once again, not all of the commodity shift can be attributed to independence.

The reports of per-capita values of exports by individual colonies and states and by major areas are of special interest. These are shown in Table 22 in real terms, to adjust for inflationary effects. It is clear that the increase in real exports from 1768–72 through the early 1790s was due almost solely to increased exports from New England and the middle Atlantic regions. Therefore, as compared with prewar proportions among the regions, it is evident that the northern areas, and especially the middle Atlantic states, gained slightly from overseas trade. This occurred despite the depression felt in Pennsylvania and New Hampshire's trade losses.

As indicated by the data on per-capita exports, the trade of the southern regions did not keep pace with their growing population. Although the South's prewar absolute level of exports had been regained by the early 1790s, per-capita exports remained significantly lower. The export trade of the northern states was a different story: except for New Hampshire, Pennsylvania, and Delaware, the new states found their export trade outpacing population. New York, especially, benefited from a prospering new agriculture.

Such widely varying fortunes among states make it unwise to generalize much about the overall effects of independence and of its economic and political pressures on market activities. It can only be said that the observable 30 percent

Table 21. *Annual average exports of selected commodities from the 13 colonies, 1768–72, and the United States, 1790–2[a]*

Commodity	Thirteen colonies 1768–72			United States, 1790–2		
	Quantity (1)	Value (£000) (2)	Value ($000: 1790–92 prices) (3)	Quantity (4)	Value ($000) (5)	Value (£000: 1768–72 prices) (6)
Beef }	26,036 bbl	51	209	60,457 bbl	367 }	159
Pork }				29,741 bbl	285 }	
Bread }	38,634 tons	410	2,534	3,823 tons	221 }	712
Flour }				63,256 tons	4,178 }	
Cotton	29,425 lb	1	7	163,822 lb	41	8
Fish, dried	308,993 quintals	154	740	375,619 quintals	900	187
Flaxseed	233,065 bu	42	189	352,079 bu	286	64
Grain:						
Corn	839,314 bu	83	424	1,926,784 bu	974	191
Rice	140,254 bbl	311	1,971	129,367 bbl	1,818	287
Wheat	599,127 bu	115	654	998,862 bu	1,090	192
Indigo	547,649 lb	113	567	493,760 lb	511	101
Iron:						
Bar	2,416 tons	36	195	300 tons	24	4
Pig	4,468 tons	22	116	3,667 tons	95	18

Livestock:						
Cattle	3,433	21	63	4,861	89	29
Horses	6,048	60	240	7,086	282	71
Naval stores:						
Pitch	11,384 bbl	5	21	7,279 bbl	13	3
Tar	90,472 bbl	34	135	68,463 bbl	102	25
Tupentine	19,870 bbl	9	42	51,194 bbl	108	24
Oil, whale	3,841 tons	46	212	1,826 tons	101	22
Potash	1,381 tons	35	134	4,872 tons	472	123
Rum, American	342,366 gal	22	132	441,782 gal	170	28
Tobacco	87,986 hhd	766	3,093	110,687 hhd	3,891	964
Wood products:						
Pine boards	38,991 M ft	70	228	45,118 M ft	264	81
Staves and headings	21,585 M	65	275	31,554 M	401	95
Total, above commodities		2,471	12,181		16,683	3,388
All exports		2,802			19,465	

[a] See the source for detailed notes on problems of comparison and measurement.

Source: Shepherd and Walton, "Economic Change after the American Revolution," pp. 408–10.

Table 22. *Average annual exports from colonies and regions of the 13 colonies, 1768–72: and states and regions of the United States, 1791–2 (Thousands of £: 1768–72 prices)*[a]

Origin	1768–72			1791–2		
	Total exports	Percent-age of total	Per-capita exports	Total exports	Percent-age of total	Per-capita exports
New England						
New Hampshire	46	2	0.74	33	1	0.23
Massachusetts	258	9	0.97	542	14	1.14
Rhode Island	81	3	1.39	119	3	1.72
Connecticut	92	3	0.50	148	4	0.62
Total, New England	477	17	0.82	842	22	0.83
Middle Atlantic						
New York	187	7	1.15	512	14	1.51
New Jersey	2	—	0.02	5	—	0.03
Pennsylvania	353	13	1.47	584	16	1.34
Delaware	18	1	0.51	26	1	0.44
Total, middle Atlantic	559	20	1.01	1,127	30	1.11
Upper South						
Maryland	392	14	1.93	482	13	1.51
Virginia	770	27	1.72	678	18	0.91
Total, upper South	1,162	41	1.79	1,160	31	1.09
Lower South						
North Carolina	75	3	0.38	104	3	0.27
South Carolina	455	16	3.66	436	12	1.75
Georgia	74	3	3.17	97	3	1.17
Total, lower South	603	22	1.75	637	17	0.88
Total, all regions	2,802	100	1.31	3,766	100	0.99

[a]See the source for detailed notes on problems of comparisons, valuations, and measurement.
Source: Shepherd and Walton, "Economic Change after the American Revolution," p. 413.

decline in aggregate real per-capita exports (per year) between 1768–72 and 1790–2 hides as much as it reveals, and that the decline in the South was probably due more to a slowing in the growth of demand for southern staples than to market alterations resulting from independence.

Although per-capita trade value had declined, the absolute volume of trade continued to rise. And this was paralleled by the growth of mercantile and shipping activities, which had been so important to the colonies (especially to New England and the middle colonies) before the war. A comparison of the pre- and postwar volume of shipping entering the colonies is shown in Table 23. Customs records indicate that the total tonnage of shipping entering U.S. ports in 1790–2 averaged 587,000 tons per year. However, an interim change in the definition of tonnage measurement calls for a downward adjustment in this figure to 406,000 tons to make it comparable with the prewar registered tonnage of ships. About 220,000 of these tons were owned in the United States, compared with 186,000 tons of foreign ownership. As can be seen from Table 23, the comparable

Table 23. *Annual average tonnages of shipping entering the 13 colonies from overseas areas, 1768–72, and the United States 1790–2, by region of entry and by domestic and foreign ownership (thousands of tons)*

Region of entry	1768–72		1790–2	
	Colonial-owned	Foreign-owned	U.S.-owned	Foreign-owned
New England	59	7	90	21
Middle Atlantic	38	13	60	61
Upper South	15	46	40	60
Lower South	8	37	30	44
Total	120	103	220	186

Source: See Table 20.

annual average tonnage entries for the prewar years were 120,000 U.S.-owned and 103,000 foreign-owned. Whether one compares the rise in the totals (from 223,000 to 406,000) or in the U.S.-owned figures (from 120,000 to 220,000), these advances approximately match or slightly exceed the population increase of 80 percent for the period.

It should be noted that part of the increase in the total tonnage entering U.S. ports resulted merely from the greater relative importance of the West Indian trade; therefore the larger total cargoes carried were offset to some extent by shorter average distances now traveled. Such alterations, however, were brought about almost totally by foreign-owned ships. For strictly U.S.-owned ships, the advance was approximately proportionate among all routes.

Therefore, unless vessel utilization or freight rates were declining, it would appear that American earnings per capita from shipping and mercantile activities had regained their prewar level by 1790. This resurgence was helpful in maintaining the strong commercial base of the northern colonies and in expediting a recovery from the doldrums of the 1780s.

Summary and conclusion

Now let us reconsider the effects of the American Revolution and of independence on the national maritime trade and, through that medium, on the overall American economy.

First, it is evident that the war interrupted a forward march begun during colonial times: a burgeoning overseas trade had been leading to growing specialization in production, to expanding agricultural productivity, and to the beginnings of urbanization and of a sound commercial base.

When that overseas trade was abruptly severed by war, the colonists were thrown back on their own devices and forced into the less economically efficient avenues of local production and self-sufficiency. Urbanization slowed for the same reason. The cities that were largest at the beginning of the war – Philadelphia, New York, and Boston – grew merely 3 percent in population between 1770 and 1790, during which time the total population of the emergent nation increased by 80 percent.

Thus the war predictably had produced economic stagnation and living standards depressed by the increasing need for self-sufficiency. But what about the period immediately following? Peace and independence called for economic as well as political reassessment. Whether the 1780s are considered as a continuation of a stagnating period or as a time of recovery from economic depression, they yielded only modest benefits to the new nation. The war-induced self-sufficiency persisted to a large degree throughout the decade, as evidenced by the data on overseas trade. The conclusion is supported, too, by contemporary evidence that agricultural productivity was on the decline in Pennsylvania (cited in Table 13). Urbanization failed to regain any momentum until after 1790.

On the brighter side, it is true that the 1780s saw the beginning of direct trade with Northern European countries other than Britain, and that these countries became important markets for American products, which no longer had to be transshipped via the mother country. Trade was also reviving with Southern Europe, and a healthily expanding West Indian trade might have become still greater except for British restrictions. This shift in relative importance of trade routes, however, was unfavorable to traditional southern staples, which were in greater demand in Northern Europe.

By the early 1790s, trade was again on the rise and total exports had climbed 40 percent above their prewar level in real terms. Since this increase was still short of the 80 percent growth of population for the period, it seems that the United States economy of that decade was far from a textbook example of economic growth led by exports. The importance of overseas trade was actually declining, both in export values per capita and as a share of income. Such a per-capita decline in peacetime was an unusual experience for any nation, although caution must again be sounded that the situation varied widely among regions. The southern decline was sharp; New York and the New England states (except New Hampshire) more than fully recovered from trade disruptions.

Such was the situation when two events in 1793 shifted the whole economic picture: the Napoleonic Wars erupted, and Eli Whitney invented the cotton gin. The sweeping consequences of those events could never have been foreseen in 1775; but even in those earlier days, as we have noted, the colonies had begun to develop the commercial base that now proved crucial. Because of its early efforts at overseas trade, the new nation was ready to take instant advantage of the economic possibilities engendered by the Napoleonic Wars.

Exceptional circumstances of that kind would come and go. But the ability to respond to them in 1793 set America on an irreversible course of industrial development that would result in standards of living undreamed of by the signers of the Declaration of Independence.

Glossary of terms

Hyperinflation
Hyperinflation is a consistent rise in the general level of prices that attains astronomical rates, such as 1,000 percent each month. Under such conditions, money may become virtually worthless, and sellers will refuse to accept it.

Putting-out system
The putting-out system, or domestic system, is a situation where businessmen deliver materials to workers who perform the production in their homes. Afterwards, the products are collected from the workers by the businessmen.

Terms of trade
The terms of trade refer to the relative prices of exports and imports. The terms of trade are said to improve when export prices increase relative to prices of imports.

Selected readings

Bjork, Gordon C., "The Weaning of the American Economy: Independence, Market Changes, and Economic Development," *Journal of Economic History*, XXIV, 4 (December 1964), pp. 541–60.

Gilbert, Geoffrey, "The Role of Breadstuffs in American Trade, 1770–1790," *Explorations in Economic History*, XIV, 4 (October 1977), pp. 378–87.

Jensen, Merrill, *The New Nation: A History of the United States during Confederation* (New York: Knopf, 1958).

Nettels, Curtis P., *The Emergence of a National Economy, 1775–1815* (New York: Holt, Rinehart and Winston, 1962), Chapters 3, 4.

North, Douglass C., *Growth and Welfare in the American Past: A New Economic History*, 2nd ed. (Englewood Cliffs, N.J.: Prentice-Hall, 1974), Chapter 5.

Shepherd, James F., and Gary M. Walton, "Economic Change after the American Revolution: Pre-War and Post-War Comparisons of Maritime Shipping and Trade," *Explorations in Economic History*, XIII, 4 (October 1976), pp. 397–422.

NOTES

Chapter 1. Introduction
1 Douglass C. North, *Growth and Welfare in the American Past,* 2nd ed. (Englewood Cliffs, N.J.: Prentice-Hall, 1974), pp. 72–3.

Chapter 2. The age of discovery and treasure
1 Of course, labor also played an indispensable part in the creation of the empires in America, but that story will be told in Chapter 3.
2 Earl J. Hamilton, "Prices as a Factor in Business Growth," *Journal of Economic History,* XII (1952), pp. 338–9.
3 For instance, the importance of American treasure has been compared to other inflationary forces, such as currency debasements. The situation for England is stated by Robert A. Doughty, "Industrial Prices and Inflation in Southern England, 1401–1640," *Explorations in Economic History,* XII (1975). Doughty's study indicates that American bullion was by no means the most important cause of the price revolution in southern England.

Chapter 3. Taking the frontier
1 Another attempt in 1607 showed similar misfortune. The Plymouth Company landed a group of settlers near the mouth of the Kennebec River in Maine, but those who survived packed up and went back to England; thus Jamestown became the first permanent British Colony in North America.
2 Charles M. Andrews, *The Colonial Period of American History,* Vol. 1 (New Haven: Yale University Press, 1934), pp. 110–11.
3 The nature of New England's comparative advantage in shipping is discussed in Chapter 4.
4 It should be pointed out, however, that vessels constructed in the colonies were typically somewhat inferior in quality compared to British-built vessels.
5 Quoted in J. Potter, "The Growth of Population in America, 1700–1860," in D.V. Glass and D.E.C. Eversley, *Population in History* (London: Edward Arnold, 1965), p. 631.
6 Abbott E. Smith, *Colonists in Bondage* (Chapel Hill: University of North Carolina Press, 1947), p. 3.

Chapter 4. The ascent of commerce

1   D.C. Coleman, "Editor's Introduction," in D.C. Coleman (ed.), *Revisions in Mercantilism* (London: Methuen, 1969), p. 4.

2   Eli F. Heckscher, *Mercantilism*, 2 vols. (London: George Allen & Unwin, 1935).

3   Jacob Viner, "Power versus Plenty as Objectives of Foreign Policy in the Seventeenth and Eighteenth Centuries," *World Politics*, I (1948), pp. 1–29; reprinted in D.C. Coleman (ed.), *Revisions in Mercantilism*, pp. 61–91.

4   See the discussion and readings in Coleman, *Revisions in Mercantilism*, for a more complete treatment of this topic.

5   W.E. Minchinton (ed.), *The Growth of English Overseas Trade in the 17th and 18th Centuries* (London: Methuen, 1969). See the Editor's Introduction, p. 9, n. 1; F.J. Fisher, "London's Export Trade in the Early Seventeenth Century," pp. 64–77; and Ralph Davis, "English Foreign Trade, 1660–1700," pp. 78–98, and "English Foreign Trade, 1700–1774," pp. 99–118.

6   Minchinton, ibid.

7   The following figures, and many of the others in this section, are from the two excellent articles by Ralph Davis cited above in note 5. The percentages are based upon average exports during 1699–1701 and 1772–4.

8   Brinley Thomas, "The Rhythm of Growth in the Atlantic Economy of the Eighteenth Century," *Research in Economic History* (forthcoming). In the above discussion we have concentrated upon discussing the broad trends of English development and trade. One might wish to see Thomas for a discussion of fluctuations in this trade during the eighteenth century

9   Great Britain, Public Record Office, Customs 16/1 (hereafter referred to as the American customs records). The detailed evidence is cited and examined in Shepherd and Walton (1972), especially in Chapters 6–8, and Appendix IV. Most of the evidence used in this section comes from this source.

10   Harvard University, Baker Library, Reynell and Coates Collection, Vol. 1, 1744–85. This invoice was received by the Philadelphia firm of Reynell and Coates on April 7, 1771, after the shipment had been delayed while the nonimportation agreements were in force.

11   Letter from Thomas Clifford, Philadelphia, to Abel Chapman, Whitby, England, July 25, 1767, quoted from Anne Bezanson et al., *Prices in Colonial Pennsylvania* (Philadelphia: University of Pennsylvania Press, 1935), p. 263.

12   The following remarks are based upon James F. Shepherd and Samuel H. Williamson, "The Coastal Trade of the British North American Colonies, 1768–1772," *Journal of Economic History*, XXXII (1972), pp. 783–810.

13   The values of coastal exports and imports should be equal, of course. There are several reasons for the discrepancies, however, primarily

that the American customs records also included the colonies of Quebec, Newfoundland, Nova Scotia, Bermuda, the Bahamas, and East and West Florida. The thirteen colonies exported more to these other colonies than they imported, according to the customs records. Moreover, the data in the records are not completely consistent.

14 The reader may wish to see Stuart Bruchey (ed.), *The Colonial Merchant: Sources and Readings* (New York: Harcourt Brace Jovanovich, 1966); or Robert A. East, *Business Enterprise in the American Revolutionary Era* (New York: Columbia University Press, 1938). For discussion of the colonial monetary system, see Joseph A. Ernst, *Money and Politics in America, 1755–1775* (Chapel Hill: University of North Carolina Press, 1973), and Leslie V. Brock, *The Currency of the American Colonies, 1700–1764* (New York: Arno Press, 1975).

15 Charles M. Andrews, "Colonial Commerce," *American Historical Review,* XX (1914), rpt. in *Readings in United States Economic and Business History,* Ross M. Robertson and James L. Pate (eds.) (Boston: Houghton Mifflin, 1966), p. 137.

16 Quoted from Harold U. Faulkner, *American Economic History* (8th ed.; New York: Harper & Row, 1960), p. 81.

17 The exception to this was the British dominance of the route between the lower South and Southern Europe. Colonial-owned ships were dominant between Great Britain and New England and the middle colonies, however.

18 Curtis P. Nettels, *The Money Supply of the American Colonies before 1720* (Madison: University of Wisconsin Studies in the Social Sciences and History, No. 20, October 1934; rpt. New York: Augustus M. Kelley, 1964), p. 70.

19 Michael Atkins, a British shipowner, in a letter to the Philadelphia merchant John Reynell in 1751 stated: "Traders at the Northern Colonies have all the West India business to themselves, Europeans can have no encouragement for mixing with them in the commodities of provisions and lumber. You time things better than we and go to market cheaper." See Richard Pares, *Yankees and Creoles* (London: Longmans, 1956), p. 8.

20 With rare exceptions, seamen were hired by the voyage out and return. See Ralph Davis, *The Rise of the English Shipping Industry* (London: Macmillan, 1962), p. 116, or the many wage contracts among the records of the High Court of Admiralty, Public Record Office, London.

21 English vessels generally engaged in little tramping and remained on regular runs "simply because among their most valuable assets were the master's and owners' connections in particular ports overseas." See Davis, pp. 196–7. For more supporting evidence and information on the risks of colonial trade, see Stuart Bruchey, "Success and Failure Factors: American Merchants in Foreign Trade in the Eighteenth and Early Nineteenth Centuries," *Business History Review,* XXXII (1958), pp. 272–92.

Chapter 5. Overseas trade and capital flows

1 Quoted from Harold U. Faulkner, *American Economic History*, 8th ed. (New York: Harper & Row, 1960), p. 81.

2 Jacob M. Price, "A Note on the Value of Colonial Exports of Shipping," *Journal of Economic History*, XXXVI (1976), pp. 704–24. The authors had earlier placed sterling exchange earnings from the sale of ships in the approximate range of £50,000 to £100,000 (Shepherd and Walton, 1972, Appendix VI, pp. 241–5). Price, using additional evidence, convincingly places such earnings at the higher level.

3 P.R.O. Customers 16/1. There are no estimates of the costs of the customs administration to Britain, but some have said the costs exceeded the customs revenues by sizable amounts. For example, John C. Miller, *Origins of the American Revolution* (Stanford: Stanford University Press, 1959), p. 83, states: "To collect two thousand pounds in customs duties in the colonies cost the British government eight thousand pounds."

4 Larry Neal, "Interpreting Power and Profit in Economic History: A Case Study of the Seven Years' War," *Journal of Economic History*, XXXVII (1977), p. 31.

5 Ship sales of £140,000 are arbitrarily assigned as £100,000 to New England and £40,000 to the middle colonies. The regional division of shipping earnings and other invisibles is derived from Shepherd and Walton (1972), Chapter 7. Because the ownership of vessels for the upper and the lower South is not given separately in the source, we can only indicate the probability that the upper South earned the greater portion of the combined £240,000 surplus.

6 Further alteration of the regional deficits and surpluses would have resulted from coastal trade among the regions. Surprisingly, however, all major regions of the thirteen colonies appear to have earned surpluses in this trade. The northern colonies of Newfoundland, Nova Scotia, and Quebec, along with Florida, the Bahamas, and the Bermuda Islands were the deficit areas. See James F. Shepherd and Samuel H. Williamson, "The Coastal Trade of the British North American Colonies, 1768–1772," *Journal of Economic History*, XXXII (1972), p. 803.

7 Great Britain, Public Record Office (Chatham Papers) 30/8/343/167, "List of Debts due by Citizens of the United States of America to the Merchants and Traders of Great Britain contracted previous to the year 1776 with interest on the same to January 1, 1790."

8 This was the rate used according to Richard B. Sheridan, "The British Credit Crisis of 1772 and the American Colonies," *Journal of Economic History*, XX (1960), pp. 166–7.

9 Aubrey C. Land, "Economic Behavior in a Planting Society: The Eighteenth-Century Chesapeake," *Journal of Southern History*, XXXIII (1967), pp. 482–3.

10 Total defense costs of the British averaged over £12 million during the Seven Years' War, and a good deal of that money is known to

have ended up in American hands. See Neal, "Interpreting Power and Profit."

11   Curtis P. Nettels, *The Money Supply of the American Colonies before 1720* (Madison, Wis.: University of Wisconsin Studies in the Social Sciences and History, No. 20, October 1934; rpt. New York: Augustus M. Kelley, 1964), p. 195. Total defense costs to Britain during these years of Queen Anne's War averaged nearly £6 million (ibid.).

12   The total official value of exports to Scotland from the colonies during this period was £1,816,318, and the value of imports was £1,546,621 (Customs 14).

Chapter 6. Productivity and economic progress

1   Herbert C. Bell, "The West India Trade before the American Revolution," *American Historical Review,* XXII (1917), p. 284.

2   Violet Barbour, "Privateers and Pirates in the West Indies," *American Historical Review,* XVI (1911), p. 529.

3   Letters of marque were the legal papers which distinguished a privateer from a pirate. Piracy was any criminal act of violence on the sea unauthorized by a governmental or political agency. Privateering was an act of warfare (or of redress, in peacetime) where private owners, officers, and crews were commissioned by a belligerent government to attack enemy vessels. The granting government typically received 10 to 15 percent of the value of prizes taken.

4   Barbour, op. cit., pp. 531–2.

5   Letters to Board of Trade, September 1, 1718, C.O. 137:13, p. 19, printed in Frank W. Pitman, *The Development of the West Indies, 1700–63* (New Haven, Conn.: Yale University Press, 1917), pp. 55–6.

6   See Barbour, op. cit., p. 566.

7   S.C. Hughson, "The Carolina Pirates and Colonial Commerce," *Johns Hopkins University Studies in Historical and Political Science* XII (1894), p. 123.

8   Ibid., p. 133.

9   Although cargoes were not always formally insured (a common practice, for example, was for colonial merchants to insure one-half the cargo and bear the remainder of the risk personally), the practice of insuring goods in shipment was common by the eighteenth century.

10   Robert E. Gallman, "Changes in Total U.S. Agricultural Factor Productivity in the Nineteenth Century," *Agricultural History,* XLVI (1972), pp. 191–210; and *idem,* "The Agricultural Sector and the Pace of Economic Growth: U.S. Experience in the Nineteenth Century," David C. Klingaman and Richard K. Vedder (eds.), *Essays in Nineteenth Century Economic History* (Athens: Ohio University Press, 1975), pp. 35–76.

11   P.W. Bidwell and J.I. Falconer, *History of Agriculture in the Northern United States 1620–1860* (Washington, D.C.: Carnegie Institution of Washington, 1925), pp. 107, 123.

12   James T. Lemon, *Best Poor Man's Country; A Geographical Study of Early*

Southeastern Pennsylvania (Baltimore: Johns Hopkins University Press, 1972), pp. 150–1.

13   Duane Ball and Gary M. Walton, "Agricultural Productivity Change in Eighteenth Century Pennsylvania," *Journal of Economic History*, XXVI, (1976), pp. 102–17.

Chapter 7. Growth and distribution of colonial income and wealth

1   Stuart Bruchey (ed.), *The Colonial Merchant: Sources and Readings* (New York: Harcourt Brace Jovanovich, 1966), p. 1.

2   Raymond W. Goldsmith, "Long Period Growth in Income and Product, 1839–1960," in Ralph L. Andreano (ed.), *New Views on American Economic Development* (Cambridge, Mass.: Schenkman, 1965), p. 355.

3   Paul A. David, "The Growth of Real Product in the United States before 1840: New Evidence, Controlled Conjectures," *Journal of Economic History*, XXVII, (1967), pp. 151–97.

4   George Rogers Taylor, "American Economic Growth before 1840: An Exploratory Essay," *Journal of Economic History*, XXIV (1964), p. 437.

5   Robert E. Gallman, "The Pace and Pattern of American Economic Growth," in Lance E. Davis et al. (eds.), *American Economic Growth: An Economist's History of the United States*, (New York: Harper & Row, 1972), pp. 19–22.

6   Phyllis Deane and W.A. Cole, *British Economic Growth, 1688–1959: Trends and Structure* (Cambridge: Cambridge University Press, 1964), p. 80.

7   Terry L. Anderson, "Wealth Estimates for the New England Colonies, 1650–1709," *Explorations in Economic History*, XII (1975), pp. 151–76.

8   Alice Hanson Jones, "Wealth Estimates for the American Middle Colonies, 1774," *Economic Development and Cultural Change*, XVIII (1970), Part 2; and "Wealth Estimates for the New England Colonies about 1770," *Journal of Economic History*, XXXII (1972), pp. 98–127.

9   Jackson Turner Main, *The Social Structure of Revolutionary America* (Princeton: Princeton University Press, 1965).

10 Robert Gallman, based upon his estimate of factor supplies (which in turn is based partly upon Jones's wealth estimates for 1774), suggests a somewhat lower range of £11 to £12½, partly because of lower wealth estimates for the middle colonies. David Klingaman, using another approach, estimates a range for per-capita output of £6½ to £19. His range is based upon estimates of the value of average per-capita consumption of basic foodstuffs (grains and meats) around 1770, and the assumption that these plus other expenditures on foodstuffs would not have been less than 40 percent nor greater than 70 percent of per-capita income. He has found that this range of expenditures on foodstuffs (as a percentage of income) is typical in many countries at different stages of development today. Although these various estimates of per-capita income do not wholly coincide, their similarity is striking, and these roughhewn but educated guesses do shed important light on questions of colonial output and living standards. Robert

E. Gallman, "The Pace and Pattern of American Economic Growth," Lance E. Davis et. al. (eds.), *American Economic Growth: An Economist's History of the United States* (New York: Harper & Row, 1972) pp. 19–22. David Klingaman, "Food Surpluses and Deficits in the American Colonies, 1768–1772," *Journal of Economic History,* XXXI (1971), pp. 553–69.

11 Alice Hanson Jones, *American Colonial Wealth: Documents and Methods* (New York: Arno Press, 1977), 3 volumes.

12 Main, *Social Structure.*

13 James Henretta, "Economic Development and Social Structure in Colonial Boston," *William and Mary Quarterly,* XXII (1965), pp. 93–105.

14 Bruce C. Daniels, "Long-Range Trends of Wealth Distribution in Eighteenth-Century New England," *Explorations in Economic History,* XI (1973–74), pp. 123–35.

15 Jackson Turner Main, "Trends in Wealth Concentrations before 1860," *Journal of Economic History,* XXXI (1971), pp. 445–7.

16 In this past century since 1860, income and wealth appear to have become more equally distributed. See Peter H. Lindert and Jeffrey G. Williamson, "Three Centuries of American Inequality," *Research in Economic History,* I (1976), pp. 69–123.

Chapter 8. British bungling and the call to arms

1 See G.M. Ostrander, "The Colonial Molasses Trade," *Agricultural History* XXX (1956), pp. 77–84, and Stuart Bruchey, *The Colonial Merchant: Sources and Readings* (New York: Harcourt Brace Jovanovich, 1966), pp. 67–78, for details of this conflict of interests.

2 Official values are not market values but, rather, reflect the volume of trade valued at fixed prices.

3 It should be noted also that trade in the Chesapeake area also was highly decentralized by comparison to other areas; this reduced the possibility of extralegal pressures and coercion (blacklisting, boycotts) from radical groups.

4 For discussion of this credit crunch, see R.B. Sheridan, "The British Credit Crisis of 1772 and the American Colonies," *Journal of Economic History,* XX (1960), pp. 161–180.

5 The situation is painfully reminiscent of the Kent State tragedy in our day: unwanted "foreign" elements of authority on someone else's home turf were goaded into overreacting to passionately expressed resentment.

6 Boston was a center of hostility largely because the new Board of Customs was centered there and because customs officials obtained their earnings from commissions on tax revenues collected. This gave them much stronger incentive to enforce the regulations and collect the taxes, in contrast to earlier agents, who had been salaried and more accommodating to the colonists.

7 It should be pointed out that the British East India Company actually served in a quasi-governmental capacity in India, and directed colonial

affairs there. It also should be noted, however, that certain members of Parliament and other powerful political interests in Britain had major portions of their personal fortunes tied to the company.

8 Smuggled Dutch tea became unprofitable because of the price decline.

9 Ross M. Robertson, *A History of the American Economy*, 3rd ed. (New York: Harcourt Brace Jovanovich, 1973).

10 See, for instance, the articles by Harper, Thomas, McClelland, and Walton in the list of references.

11 Lawrence A. Harper, "The Effect of the Navigation Acts on the Thirteen Colonies," in Richard B. Morris (ed.), *The Era of the American Revolution* (New York: Columbia University Press, 1939; reprinted by Harper Torchbooks, 1965), pp. 3–39.

12 Roger Ransom, "British Policy and Colonial Growth: Some Implications of the Burdens of the Navigation Acts," *Journal of Economic History*, XXVII (1968), p. 434.

13 L.C. Gray, *A History of Agriculture in the Southern United States to 1860* (Baltimore: Waverly Press, 1933), p. 258.

14 Lawrence A. Harper, "Mercantilism and the American Revolution," *Canadian Historical Review*, XXV (1942), p. 13.

15 Charles Andrews, "The American Revolution: An Interpretation," *American Historical Review*, XXXI (1926), p. 232.

16 Harper (1942), p. 14.

Chapter 9. Economic prospects for the new republic

1 Anne Bezanson et al., *Prices and Inflation during the American Revolution: Pennsylvania, 1770–1790* (Philadelphia: University of Pennsylvania Press, 1951), p. 17.

2 Gordon Bjork, "The Weaning of the American Economy: Independence, Market Changes, and Economic Development," *Journal of Economic History*, XXIV (1964), p. 548.

3 *The Federalist,* Paper 15.

4 It is important to recall that the issue of the distribution of wealth took on a wider focus than that concerning the mere control of the money stock. Indeed, maintenance of the distribution of wealth (or at least the establishment of barriers to prevent significant and radical changes in the distribution of wealth through government channels) was an issue of sensitive concern to the writers of the Federalist Papers. In Paper 10 James Madison brings into sharp focus his preoccupation with these important matters and his concern about "factions" and the limits of majority rule: "The most common and durable source of factions has been the various and unequal distribution of property. Those who hold and those who are without property have ever formed distinct interests in society. Those who are creditors, and those who are debtors, fall under a like discrimination. A landed interest, a manufacturing interest, a mercantile interest, a money interest, with many lesser interests, grow up of necessity in civilized nations, and divide them into different classes, actuated by different senti-

ments and views. The regulation of these various and interfering interests forms the principal task of modern legislation, and involves the spirit of party and faction in the necessary and ordinary operations of the government. . . . The inference to which we are brought is, that the causes of faction cannot be removed, and that relief is only to be sought in the means of controlling its effects.

If a faction consists of less than a majority, relief is supplied by the republican principle, which enables the majority to defeat its sinister views by regular vote. It may clog the administration, it may convulse the society; but it will be unable to execute and mask its violence under the forms of the Constitution. When a majority is included in a faction, the form of popular government, on the other hand, enables it to sacrifice to its ruling passion or interest both the public good and the rights of other citizens. To secure the public good and private rights against the danger of such a faction, and at the same time to preserve the spirit and the form of popular government, is then the great object to which our inquiries are directed."

5   Thomas Jefferson described at length the urgent need for strong economic diplomacy in hurdling the trade barriers which blocked American overseas commerce before and shortly after the adoption of the Constitution.

First. In Europe –
Our breadstuff is at most times under prohibitory duties in England, and considerably dutied on re-exportation from Spain to her colonies.
Our tobaccos are heavily dutied in England, Sweden, France, and prohibited in Spain and Portugal.
Our rice is heavily dutied in England and Sweden and prohibited in Portugal.
Our fish and salted provisions are prohibited in England, and under prohibitory duties in France.
Our whale oils are prohibited in England and Portugal. And our vessels are denied naturalization in England, and of late, in France.

Second. In the West Indies –
All intercourse is prohibited with the possessions of Spain and Portugal.
Our salted provisions and fish are prohibited by England.
Our salted pork and breadstuff (except maize) are received under temporary laws only in the dominions of France, and our salted fish pays there a weighty duty.

Third. In the article of navigation –
Our own carriage of our own tobacco is heavily dutied in Sweden, and lately in France.
We can carry no article, not of our own production, to the British ports in Europe. Nor even our own produce to her American possessions.

...Our ships, though purchased and navigated by their own subjects, are not permitted to be used, even in their trade with us. ...

Our vessels pay in their ports one shilling and nine pence, sterling, per ton, light and trinity dues, more than is paid by British ships, except in the port of London, where they pay the same as British. The greater part of what they receive from us is re-exported to other countries, under the useless charges of an intermediate deposite, and double voyage.

Thomas Jefferson, "Report of Secretary of State on the privileges and restrictions on the commerce of the United States in foreign countries," Report to the 3rd Cong., 1st Sess., December 16, 1793, printed in *American State Papers,* 1789–1794, I (Boston, 1817), pp. 431–2; 428.

6   For example, Robertson's widely used text states: "During the 1790s tobacco continued to head the list of American exports in dollar value ... " Ross M. Robertson, *A History of the American Economy,* 3rd ed. (New York: Harcourt Brace Jovanovich, 1973), p. 115.

7   Bjork, "The Weaning of the American Economy," p. 544.

8   See, for instance, Robert P. Thomas, "A Quantitative Approach to the Study of the Effects of British Imperial Policy upon Colonial Welfare: Some Preliminary Findings," *Journal of Economic History,* XXV (1965), p. 628. Indigo exports fell to negligible levels by the mid–1790s, however, due to the competition of British West Indian production.

INDEX

Act of Union (1707), 74
Acts of Trade, 173, 174, 175
admiralty courts: Navigation Acts, 158; smuggling, 161
Africa: Atlantic economies, 16, 18; colonial trade, 79, 80, 86; Portugese and, 12–13; trade credits, 99; triangles of trade, 90, 91
African Company, 35
aggregate demand: definition, 28–9; increase in, 18
agrarian capitalism, 34
agriculture (America): colonial patterns in, 42, 114; dominance of, 49–50; European crops and stock in, 33; intensive, 45; parttime manufacture, 133; productivity changes, 130–6, 138
agriculture (Europe): English, 69; population and, 17; prices, 26
American Customs Board, 167
American Revolution, 42, 109, 160 agricultural productivity, 133; capitalism, 170, 175; credit/debt structures, 98, 108; economic consequences of, 198–200; economic development, 4; exploitation, 170–5; French power, 162; income and wealth levels at, 142, 148; mercantilism, 68; merchants, 3; money supply, 89; population at, 53; trade patterns and, 78, 87, 175, 178–82
Amsterdam, colonial trade, 77, 177
Anderson, Terry, 141, 152
Andrews, Charles, 37–8, 176
Antwerp (Belgium), 17–18, 19
apprenticeship, 58, 114

Arguian, 13
Armada (Spanish), 27, 70
armaments, naval, 120, 125, 126, 128
army (British), balance of payments, 102–3, 109
Articles of Confederation, 186, 187
artisans, 182; colonial economy, 49
Ashley, Lord, 41
Asia: joint stock companies, 35; long-distance trade, 10
Astor, John Jacob, 2
Azores: Portugese exploration, 12; sugar production, 13

Bahamas, native populations, 32
balance-of-payments: colonial trade, 85, 94, 99–103; defined, 6; money supply and, 105; Napoleonic wars, 1, 2; statistics of, 101
balance of trade: deficit, 97; defined, 94; mercantilism, 64, 96
Ball, Duane, 132, 137
Baltic trade, 17, 119, 125
Baltimore (Md.), expansion, 2, 48
Baltimore, Lord (Sir George Calvert), 41
banks, 104, 172
Barbados trade, port time, 123
Barbary pirates, 183, 187; see also pirates and privateers
Barbour, Violet, 126
Bateman, Fred, x
beef, see livestock
Bell, Herbert C., 115
Bezanson, Anne, 117, 182
Bidwell, P. W., 63
Bight of Biafra, 13

children: settlements, 33; textiles, 49
China, long-distance trade, 10
Christianity, 31, 32, 33
Church (Spanish), 31
Cipolla, Carlo M., 30
Civil War (English), 66, 78
clothing, colonial markets, 83
coal production, 69, 71
coastal trade, 87–8; revolution, 181; ship size, 119, 120
cocoa, trade, 3
codfish, mercantilism, 75
Coelho, Philip, x
coffee trade, 3, 86
Coleman, D. C., 95
colonization, mercantilism, 36, 40
Columbus, Christopher, 19, 20, 33; voyages, 9, 10, 14–15
commerce (American): economic development, 6; Napoleonic wars, 3, 4
commerce (European): England, 70; growth of, 27
commercialization, concentration of wealth, 149–50
commercial organization: Dutch East India Company, 16; Italian trade, 14; *see also* business organization
commercial sector: agriculture, 50; coastal trade, 88; defined, 7; development of, 47, 94, 115, 148; Napoleonic wars, 2; postwar economy, 198, 200
Committees of Correspondence, American Revolution, 175
commodity exports, *see* exports
commodity trade, 28; statistics of, 98, 99
communications: colonial governments, 155–6; marketing, 92, 115
comparative advantage: definition, 62; specialization, 115; sugar production, 46
Confederation period, population growth, 186
Connecticut: exports, 46; government of, 154; wealth in, 149
Constitution (U.S.): economy, 186; taxation, 187; trade, 188, 189
Continental Congress, 169, 179
copper, 18, 71, 83

correspondent relationships, 89
Cortes, Hernando, 20, 32
cotton, colonial production, 3, 86
cotton gin, 193
courts: admiralty, 158, 161; duty enforcement, 167; indentured servitude, 58, 59; vice-admiralty, 167
Covilhão, Pedro de, 15
craftsmen, colonial economy, 49
credit: colonial trade, 89–90, 105, 158; cost of, 130; market facilities, 94; overextension of, 167; postwar, 184
crew size: productivity, 119, 120; technology, 125
Cromwell's Protectorate: mercantilism, 66; proprietary colonies, 41
crops, European in America, 33
Crown (British): colonial governments, 154, 155; colonization, 36, 38; trade restrictions, 68, 96
Crown (Spanish), encomienda, 31
Crown colonies, English settlements, 40–1
Cuba, 180; native populations, 32; Spanish settlements, 20
currency: Constitution, 187; Continental, 181; markets, 124
Currency Act (1751), 172, 175
currency regulation, British, 170, 172–3
customs duties, balance of payments, 102

da Gama, Vasco, 12–13, 15
Damascus, long-distance trade, 10
Daniels, Bruce C., 148, 149
d'Avenal, Comte, 25
David, Paul, 140, 152
Davis, Ralph, 30, 63, 70, 71
debt(s): American Revolution, 106; British claims for, 107–8; currency regulation, 172; increase in, 110; slavery, 102; trade patterns, 97, 98, 103–8
Declaration of Independence, 175, 200
Declaratory Act, 166
defense: balance of payments, 97, 102, 103, 106, 109; colonial trade, 174
Delaware: iron production, 160; proprietary colony, 41

224   *Index*

skills: immigrants, 69–70; productivity, 113, 114
slaves and slavery: containment, 59–60; encomienda practice compared, 32; Georgia, 60–1; indentured servitude, 58–9; personal wealth statistics and, 146; Portugese exploration, 13; purchases of, 106, 135; sugar plantations, 34, 73
slave trade, 86; American revolution, 180; Atlantic economies, 16; colonial trade, 80; England, 35; fifteenth century, 13; mercantilism, 74, 75; population, 55; Portugal, 14; trade deficits, 100, 101, 102; triangles of trade, 90
Smith, Abbott E., 57
Smith, Adam, ii, 65, 114
smuggling: Navigation Acts, 158; sugar, 161; vice-admiralty courts, 167; wartime, 178
South (American): black population, 55–7; wealth in, 143, 146, 150; *see also* lower South; southern colonies; upper South
South Carolina: black population, 56; exports, 185; rice production, 44
southern colonies: debts in, 106–7; English trade, 80–1, 88; indentured servitude, 58; personal wealth distribution, 147–8; trade deficit, 97
Southern Europe: colonial markets, 75, 99, 104, 110, 158; exports to, 79, 80, 81; imports of, 47, 83, 85; middle colony market, 46; postwar trade, 191, 199; triangular trade, 90
Southern States, postwar economy, 184
Spain: American dominions, 20–2, Canary influence of, 16; explorations of, 9, 11–12, 20, 31–4; food imports by, 17; postwar trade of, 182, 183, 185; prices in, 22; real wages, 23; Revolutionary War trade, 179, 180, 181; silver, 19, 27; tobacco exports, 38
Spanish America, commercial development, 47
Spanish Armada (1588), defeat of, 27, 70

Spanish dollar, 89
Spanish Florida, 60
specialization: postwar, 198; regions, 5, 114–15, 138, 139
spices, 16; trade in, 3; long-distance trades, 11
Stamp Act (1765), 68, 175, 176; colonial reaction, 165; repealed, 166
Stamp Act Congress, 165
standard of living, *see* living standards
Staple Act (1663), 173
starving time, 35, 37–8
steel production, restricted, 160
storage, *see* warehousing
subsistence agriculture, equality, 149; extent of, 42; lower South, 44; market economy, 6; natural tariffs, 115; persistence of, 50
Sugar Act (1764): mercantilism, 68; provisions of, 164
sugar plantations: black slavery, 13, 33, 34; economic specialization, 46, 81; Portugese, 14; settlement patterns, 34
sugar trade, 3; Atlantic economies, 16; colonial markets, 33, 42, 86; mercantilism, 72–3; northern Europe, 18; Portugal, 14; reexports trade, 72; triangles of trade, 90
surpluses, settlement stages, 139
Sutch, Richard, x

tariffs, Constitution, 188
tariff rebates, reexport trade, 164
taxation: Articles of Confederation, 187; collection of, 164, 167; colonial share, 163–4; external, 164–5, 176, 177; per-capita burdens (1765), 163; property (British), 167; reexports, 158
Taylor, George Rogers, 140–1, 152
tea: colonial markets, 85; duties on, 167, 168–9; prices, 174
Tea Act, 175
technical diffusion: definition, 137; technology, 113
technological change, definition, 137
technology: agriculture, 114; distribution costs, 130; English economy, 69; productivity, 113; ships and shipping, 124–5